Israel and the Neoconservatives

Israel and the Neoconservatives

Zionism and American Interests

Adam L. Fuller

LEXINGTON BOOKS
Lanham • Boulder • New York • London

Published by Lexington Books
An imprint of The Rowman & Littlefield Publishing Group, Inc.
4501 Forbes Boulevard, Suite 200, Lanham, Maryland 20706
www.rowman.com

6 Tinworth Street, London SE11 5AL

Copyright © 2020 by The Rowman & Littlefield Publishing Group, Inc.

All rights reserved. No part of this book may be reproduced in any form or by any electronic or mechanical means, including information storage and retrieval systems, without written permission from the publisher, except by a reviewer who may quote passages in a review.

British Library Cataloguing in Publication Information Available

Library of Congress Cataloging-in-Publication Data Available

ISBN 978-1-4985-6733-6 (cloth)
ISBN 978-1-4985-6735-0(pbk)
ISBN 978-1-4985-6734-3 (electronic)

Contents

Preface	vii
Introduction	1
1 Because they are Zionists?	5
2 More Concern for Israel's Interests Than America's?	23
3 More Concern About Liberal Democracy?	37
4 Because They Are American Jews	49
5 Looking Ahead	61
Bibliography	89
Index	95
About the Author	99

Preface

This project began as a paper I delivered at the Lisa and Michael Leffell Foundation's colloquium on "The Impact of Israel on American Jewry." The conference was held in 2016 in White Plains, New York. It was an interdisciplinary meeting with academics across the United States and Israel discussing academically the ways that Israel affects Jews in America and the problems that lay ahead in the two countries' relationship. Topics ranged from the origins of American Zionism, the possible replacement of Israel with *Tikkun Olam* as a source of Jewish meaning in American Jewish communities, the incorporation of Israeli culture into American *yiddishkeit*, the portrayal of Israel in American Jewish media, the fragmentation of the Israel lobby, the decline of American Jewish youth attachment to Israel, and thoughts on new methods of American education about Israel.

Having previously written *Taking the Fight to the Enemy: Neoconservatism and the Age of Ideology*, also published by this house in 2012, my contribution to the seminar was to deliver my thoughts on the neoconservatives, an influential wing within the Republican Party that is largely comprised of Jews. I wanted to analyze why they support the Jewish state and in what direction they try to steer America's Israel policy. Many myths and misconceptions about this movement need to be straightened out. I believed the subject warranted a lengthier, expanded analysis.

When the paper was presented and discussed at that conference, the 2016 election had not yet concluded. Most of the discussion about the future of American and Israeli politics assumed that Hillary Clinton was going to be our 45th president. The Trump election was a surprise to many people interested in making forecasts of the future of America's relationship with Israel. As many neoconservatives supported Mrs. Clinton and continue to denounce

Trumpism in the GOP, it certainly has altered the future of this particular form of conservatism, for better or worse.

At the colloquium, there was also a lot of discussion about creating an academic subfield about "The Impact of Israel on American Jewry." Of what discipline it would be a subfield within is hard to say, but it is a certainly an important and worthwhile interdisciplinary focus. This is especially true as American Jewish attitudes about the Jewish state morph with each passing generation. It is currently the spring of 2019 and all of the events discussed in the forthcoming pages reflect what I know at this moment in time. The next generation of neoconservatives, if there are any left in a few decades, may even look upon Israel in a different manner than the way it is described here.

I would like to acknowledge the Lisa and Michael Leffell Foundation for their research grant for this project and for compelling me to undertake it. Thanks should also be extended to all of my colleagues at that seminar. In addition, I would like to acknowledge the support of my colleagues in the Department of Politics and International Relations and our Center for Judaic and Holocaust Studies at Youngstown State University—who have all been valuable intellectual sounding boards during my research. I must also thank my friend David Frisk at the Alexander Hamilton Institute for the Study of Western Civilization, a great thinker in all things intellectually conservative, for his constant help. Thanks should also go to the Schusterman Center for Israel Studies at Brandeis University, for including me as a fellow in their summer institute in Israel. Participation with the Schusterman Center has been very valuable opportunity in helping me develop greater knowledge about the Jewish state so that I can be a better teacher and scholar of Israeli politics. Lastly, I must also acknowledge some of the figures discussed here, for letting me interview them for this project: Norman Podhoretz, Joshua Muravhick, and Paul Gottfried.

Introduction

In the pages of *Commentary* magazine and *The Weekly Standard*, neoconservatives argue almost every day on behalf of the Jewish state. If there is one consistent policy message neoconservatives espouse, it is that it is imperative for U.S. foreign policy to support Israel's existential defense crisis. More especially, neoconservatives usually favor support of Israel's center-right Likud Party. While neoconservatives vary in their views on other issues, this is the one policy area in which they always seem to be in full agreement. While there are gentile neoconservatives, the movement's sociological origin is in the New York Jewish Intellectual circle, when in the 1960s several among them became disillusioned by the Left and moved to the political Right. It is safe to say that when speaking of "neoconservatives," we are primarily talking about Jewish Americans. Prominent neoconservatives include Irving Kristol, William Kristol, Norman Podhoretz, Midge Decter, John Podhoretz, Robert Kagan, Donald Kagan, Richard Perle, Joshua Muravchik, David Horowitz, Charles Krauthammer, David Frum, Hillel Halkin, David Brooks, Jonathan Tobin, Max Boot, Bret Stephens, Paul Wolfowitz, Douglas Feith, and Elliot Abrams. Mostly supporters of the Republican Party, some Democrats, such as former Senator Joseph Lieberman and other "Scoop Jackson" Democrats, can be added into the mix.

Norman Podhoretz once wrote:

> While the general impression that all neo-conservatives are Jewish is false, it is certainly true that all neo-conservatives are strong supporters of Israel. This has as much—and in many cases more—to do with the fact that Israel is a democratic state as that it is a Jewish one. For whereas neo-conservatives may differ among themselves over the extent and nature of American commitments abroad, they would all agree that at a minimum the United States has a vital interest in the survival of the relatively few democratic states already in exis-

tence. Israel, in particular, is seen by neo-conservatives as the most exposed of the democracies—the loneliest outpost of what they insist on calling (in deliberate defiance of the ridicule that has been heaped on the term in recent years) the free world.[1]

That simple explanation unfortunately is not enough for the critics of neoconservatism to understand their interest in the Jewish state. The question of why they support Israel, and in particular, its Likud Party, is the subject of interest to many cynical doubters, conspiracy theorists, and just run-of-the-mill pundits and academics. The usual answer is that neoconservatives, being Jews, feel a tribal attachment to their homeland. This answer has often led to allegations of American disloyalty, but not everyone who answers it in this way is necessarily alleging anything sinister. However, it is not the only answer. It has also been suggested that the neoconservatives' support for Israel is not even driven by their own Jewishness at all, but rather by their American liberal democratic sensibilities. To some, neoconservatives are Zionist Jews who pledge a higher allegiance to a foreign country than their own. To others, they are jingoistic, chest pounding American zealots who are only interested in waging war to assert America's "national greatness."

These are caricatures, so a more tempered analysis is in order. Neoconservatives view Israel's political tradition as combining two elements: (1) Jewishness, and (2) freedom. Israel, being a country where rights are afforded to its citizens, holds free and fair elections, and has dynamic capitalist enterprise, enjoys a uniquely Jewish-American experience. Because Israel is the only state in the region with any of these characteristics, the country is of paramount concern to neoconservatives and they feel should also be important to America. Israel, then, is an extension of American exceptionalism, and one that for many Jewish Americans is a source of pride. It thus becomes a rational political imperative for American Jews to lend support to the Jewish state. Their "American *Yiddishkeit*" combines the best of both being American and being Jewish. Thus, they consider a pro-Israel agenda a noble priority.

The purpose of this book is not to argue in support of a close American-Israeli alliance based on the neoconservative model. Their view of Israel is more of an ideal than the actual reality, and they exaggerate Jewish state's compatibility with the "American idea." The case could also certainly be made that the United States too often supersedes its own interests for the sake of Israeli security and that less of an entanglement between the United States and Israel would even serve both countries better. However, for the sake of a fair, honest debate on U.S. foreign policy, it is essential that academics, journalists, policymakers, and the public recognize that neoconservatism is a legitimate paradigm and that the people who espouse it are not actually seeking to subvert their own country's interests for the sake of another's.

Since there are so many misconceptions and, in many cases, conspiracy theories, surrounding the neoconservatives and their intentions, this book will begin with them.

NOTE

1. Norman Podhoretz, "The Neoconservative Anguish Over Reagan's Foreign Policy," *New York Times*, May 2, 1982.

Chapter One

Because they are Zionists?

In the forward to Stephen J. Sniegoski's *The Transparent Cabal*, former Illinois Congressman Paul Findlay assures readers that, "In spite of charges to the contrary, the term 'neocon' is not a code word for 'Jew.'" Findlay then says, "But the fact is, as author Philip Weiss points out, the neoconservatives originated as a largely Jewish movement in the 1970s 'in good part out of concern for Israel's security.'"[1] Findlay adds, "At the same time, a fear of being smeared with the 'anti-Semite' label should not, and does not, prohibit Dr. Sniegoski from pointing out the fact that people—all people—are affected to a greater or lesser degree in their foreign policy views by ethnic and emotional ties to a foreign country (often the country of the forebears)."[2]

Findlay exaggerates the extent to which "concern for Israel's security" played a role in the origins of neoconservatism. While *Commentary* magazine was published by the American Jewish Committee and indeed had pro-Israel leanings, neoconservatives arose out of a far greater milieu of causes. Moreover, there are many gentile neoconservatives, such as James Q. Wilson, Peter Berger, Edward Banfield, Senator Daniel Patrick Moynihan, Jeanne Kirkpatrick, Francis Fukuyama, William Bennett, and Donald Rumsfeld. As R. Emmett Tyrell puts it in *The Conservative Crack-Up*, "A barbarous world was being thrust upon these neoconservatives, and they chose to resist. . . . Reality was being transformed, and its unpleasant features were being thrust upon those who cared deeply about freedom and democracy." Not everyone who was concerned about the crisis of the west went the route of neoconservatism, but many did. Tyrell adds: "Israel's catalytic role in turning many a Liberal into a neoconservative gave birth to the myth that neoconservatives were mostly fearful Zionists alarmed over Israel's fate."[3]

It is not just issues directly related to Israel that neoconservatives are accused of nudging U.S. foreign policy toward Israel's support. Nearly every issue related to the Middle East—such as the Persian Gulf War, the Iraq War, Iranian nuclear proliferation, and the Syrian civil war—are only some of the major issues of Middle Eastern regional theater in which the neoconservatives are accused of pushing a U.S. policy toward the benefit of Israel. Sniegoski makes this case in *The Transparent Cabal*, as do Stephen Walt and John Mearsheimer in their book and *London Review of Books* paper, *The Israel Lobby*, in which they write, "Given the neo-conservatives' devotion to Israel, their obsession with Iraq, and their influence in the Bush administration, it isn't surprising that many Americans suspected that the war was designed to further Israeli interests."[4] This book does not seek to challenge that component, but it does challenge the meme that they are only doing so out of a tribal attachment to the Jewish homeland.

"Neoconservatism" is a term that is nowadays understood as an interventionist U.S. foreign policy paradigm, but as a strain of the American Right, it did not begin that way. Originally composed of former leftist anti-communists who became disillusioned by the Great Society of the 1960s and the Democratic Party's shift toward internationalism in the 1970s, the "neoconservative circle" realigned with the Republican Party in the 1980s. A major force in the Reagan administration, the neoconservatives were also vital architects of the "Contract with America" in the 1990s and later a major influence on the administration of George W. Bush. In the 1980s, there was some interest in the neoconservatives, beginning with Peter Steinfels' book, *The Neoconservatives: The Men Who Are Changing America's Politics*, but they were not examined quite critically until the 1990s. Shadia Drury's *Leo Strauss and the American Right* was an important tome at that time criticizing the movement's domestic agenda.

The Jewish political theorist of the Left, Michael Walzer, suggests that what primarily motivates the neoconservatives as Jewish actors is not so much Jewish values or a Jewish way of life, but Jewish interests, and narrowly defined ones at that. In an essay in *Dissent*, responding to Podhoretz's book, *Why Are Jews Liberal?*, Walzer writes, "Contemporary Jewish neoconservatism can be seen as an effort to embrace this interest group status and then, since it is after all a considerable comedown from the Congregation of Israel, to recoup some pride by insisting on a fierce defense of Jewish interests." He goes on to add, "But not all that much pride can be recouped, it seems to me, since this is mostly a defense of our interests against people who are weaker than we are, and since it is a defense of our interests in the narrowest sense."[5] For Walzer, whether the issue is the domestic economy, social policy, or the Israeli-Palestinian conflict, neoconservatives abandon the values of Jewishness and think rather of Jews as those who need to have their rights protected. A similar formula could, for Walzer, also be at work in explaining contemporary Christian conservatism. Walzer believes that most American Jews reject neoconservatism—or any form of conservatism at all—because they believe that Jewish interests are tied more closely to a Jewish value of social justice. As it will be shown later, however, Walzer's premise that neoconservatism is value-free could not be further from the truth. Neoconservatives most definitely are concerned with liberal democratic values, just a very differently defined set of values than the social justice Walzer is describing. Their focus on values is, in fact, why they are so heavily associated, rightly or wrongly, with Leo Strauss.

While most of the criticism has come from the Left, there are traditionalist conservatives, known as "paleoconservatives," who have unified in reaction to the neoconservatives' perceived dominance of the Republican Party agenda. And while most of the criticism does indeed come from the Left, a lot of the accusations about the conspiracy of the Jewish lobby began with the paleoconservatives were subsequently adopted by the Left, which Norman Podhoretz correctly argues in his book, *World War IV*.[6] Although they are unconcerned about left-wing politics, the paleoconservatives believe that this "cabal" has nudged the Republican Party—the party they do care about—toward supporting Israel even against American interests. They are therefore only too happy to see neoconservatives admonished by left-wing pundits and professors as well.

Paleoconservatives certainly add an important dimension to conservative political thinking and on a whole host of subjects provide insights on problems that are largely ignored by today's conservative and libertarian establishment. However, paleoconservatives have become so associated with "anti-Israel conservatism" that it has seemingly become their defining characteristic. True or not, one associates them with opposition to Israel in the way that being "pro-Israel" seems to have defined the neoconservatives. Their weekly magazine, *The American Conservative*, devotes abundant space to criticizing America's relationship with Israel. Interestingly, its founding editor, Scott McConnell, was actually Norman Podhoretz's protégé at *Commentary* before breaking ranks on him.[7] McConnell thinks the neoconservatives have vastly elevated Israel's importance and expect every American to do the same. He writes: "As an American, one is never asked simply to like or respect Israel as a foreign country—one is asked to more or less worship the place."[8]

Certainly not all paleoconservatives are opposed to America's alliance with Israel. Most of them do not write about the issue at all, or if they do, it is very little. The most hostile to Israel have been Joseph Sobran, Robert Novak, Paul Craig Roberts, and Patrick J. Buchanan. Sobran's vociferous opposition to the neoconservatives earned him a dismissal from *National Review*'s masthead. The *Washington Post* columnist Bob Novak, a Jewish-born convert to Catholicism, referred to Israel's treatment of Palestinians as "worse than Apartheid"[9] and vehemently disliked Bush's neoconservative policy advisors. Roberts is the author of many articles and books, including, *The*

Neoconservative Threat to World Order, in which he argues that the neoconservative agenda is bringing the world to the brink of nuclear war. He writes, "The neocon scum and crazed Israeli government have worked for years, together with the idiot Republican Party to create a false reality about Iran and nonexistent nuclear weapons program in the hope of starting a war with Iran."[10] As for Buchanan, he was at one time an ally of neoconservatives when he worked with some of them in the Nixon administration but later became one of their fiercest opponents.

A lukewarm critic is Russell Kirk, an important conservative thinker of the traditionalist variety. In 1988, Kirk told an audience at the Heritage Foundation, "Not seldom has it seemed as if some eminent neoconservatives mistook Tel Aviv for the capital of the United States."[11] Midge Decter was in the audience and was offended by Kirk's allegation. The incendiary remark remains controversial, although put into the context of the rest of his speech, it is not necessarily anti-Semitic. Kirk did credit the neoconservatives in that same speech for improving upon pre-established U.S. foreign policy paradigms in other regions of the world, particularly in the Asian theater, but strongly disagreed with the path they wanted to take the United States down in Middle Eastern geopolitics. He did regard their influence on Reagan as being too supportive of Israel at the expense of American interests.

Far more provocative than that was when Pat Buchanan said on PBS's *McLaughlin Group*, "Capitol Hill is Israeli Occupied Territory."[12] In *Dead Right*, David Frum describes Buchanan's allegation with sarcasm:

> To Patrick Buchanan, the Gulf War offered the sublime opportunity to reenact the Great Debate of 1940–1941. In the role of Britain—slyly manipulating U.S. politics to maneuver American boys into fighting its wars—was Israel. Playing the part of the striped-pants boys around Colonel Stimpson were the Jewish neoconservatives of New York and Washington. City College stood in for the Groton as the training-ground for internationalists who owed their loyalty to a foreign power. Buchanan himself would revive the boffo box-office performance of Charles A. Lindbergh.[13]

Frum continues: "Buchanan ominously ticked off the names of Jewish advocates of war: Kissinger and Krauthammer, Rosenthal and Perle. And as Lindbergh had claimed that Jews were a 'danger' to the United States because of 'their large ownership and influence in our motion pictures, our press, our radio, and our government,' so Buchanan decried the excessive influence within the conservative movement of the hated neocons."[14] Frum may very well be right that history is repeating itself with Buchanan as a modern-day Lindbergh. In a letter to William F. Buckley, Irving Kristol told him that Buchanan is "politically anti-Semitic" as opposed to "personally anti-Semitic."[15] Kristol meant that while Buchanan gets along fine with Jews on an individual basis, he thinks that there is a concerted political effort amongst American Jewry to subvert U.S. interests in favor of Israel's and is particularly vexed by what Jews are doing to corrupt the conservative movement.

In the pages of *National Review* (*NR*), the flagship magazine of the conservative movement, founded by Buckley, there were some writers who were expressing strongly anti-Israel sentiments. By the 1980s and 1990s, some of these were openly critical of the Jewish neoconservative influence on the Reagan administration's Middle East policies. The most ardent of these columnists was Sobran, who by his final years was an open Holocaust revisionist[16] and blamed America's Israel policy for the 9/11 attacks.[17] Although he was always bemoaning "Zionist power," the extreme level of his dislike for that power exacerbated throughout the two decades following his expulsion from *NR*.

Buckley expunged Sobran from the masthead, informing him that there have been many reader complaints. Buckley stated in his book, *In Search of Anti-Semitism*, that some of these complaints were from *NR*'s neoconservative allies. Norman Podhoretz, for example, referred to Sobran's columns about the "real" motivations for the Gulf War as "contextually anti-Semitic."[18] This dismissal—especially for the reason given—only made Sobran even more furious about the "Zionist power" over freedom of the press and the double standard that, "If a Jew complains about Christians, Christians must be persecuting him. If a Christian complains about Jews, he is doing the persecuting—in the very act of complaining."[19] In a 2016 *Commentary* essay, Stephen B. Smith suggests that Leo Strauss's 1957 letter to the editor prompted Buckley's purge of anti-Semites in *NR*.[20] In that letter, Strauss answered the charge on behalf of Israel that it is a racist state.

Sobran also called Buckley's decision to fire him a "failure of nerve." He accused Buckley of bucking to Jewish "retaliatory power."[21] Father Richard John Neuhaus, editor of *First Things*, was incensed that *National Review* under the editorship of John O'Sullivan endorsed Pat Buchanan's candidacy against the incumbent George H.W. Bush in 1992 merely because he was the only candidate challenging Bush from the Right. Neuhaus and his cohort alleged that Buchanan was anti-Semitic and should not have be receiving *NR*'s endorsement even for the tactical reasons O'Sullivan cited. Writers at *Chronicles* magazine were furious at Buckley for acquiescing to the neoconservative anti-Semite-baiting of Buchanan and Sobran. Neuhaus argued that *Chronicles* was playing a double game, akin to saying, "We and our friends are not anti-Semitic, and anybody who says otherwise is a tool of the Jewish conspiracy."[22]

Sobran and Buchanan both also believed that it was the power of the Jewish neoconservatives that had steered Christian conservatives away from the essential principles of conservatism. It is a common paleoconservative criticism of the neoconservatives that they are, as James Burnham put it,

"Still living in an emotional gestalt of liberalism" and that their influence in movement conservatism have merged left-wing visions with the political Right.[23] Many of the Republican neoconservatives were, in fact, once either Democrats or even radical Leftists in their younger days. Although, this is also true of several prominent Christian conservative public intellectuals such as Burnham, Whittaker Chambers, and others, who are not neoconservatives. Buckley and other significant Christian conservatives figures, paleoconservatives believe, have been co-opted into tempering their conservative views by the neoconservative establishment. Burnham, of course, was not specifically talking about their influence on America's Israel policy and did not appear to be attributing his assertion to their Jewishness. However, Sobran certainly did. Sobran writes:

> I couldn't understand what the fuss was about. I'd merely applied conservative principles—the things *National Review* stood for—to Israel: it was a socialist country with no conception of limited, constitutional government, which discriminated against Christians, while betraying its benefactor, the United States, and turning the Muslim world against us. It seemed pretty clear-cut to me, and none of the reasons conservatives gave for supporting Israel made much sense.[24]

Another rift within neoconservative camps itself, between David Horowitz and William Kristol. Horowitz had written a piece for *Breitbart* in which he said, "I am a Jew who has never been to Israel and has never been a Zionist in the sense of believing that Jews can rid themselves of Jew hatred by having their own nation state. I am also an American (and an American first), whose country is threatened with destruction by the same enemies."[25] In and of itself, this comment is not anything with which Kristol would disagree, but the *Breitbart* piece was directed at him, accusing him and the "Never Trump" lobby of abandoning the one political party that fiercely stands up against both America and Israel's mutual enemies.

What caused the piece to get mainstream media attention was the provocative headline, "Bill Kristol: Republican Spoiler, Renegade Jew?"[26] It went "viral" on social media, and columnists both Left and Right denounced Horowitz's piece and lamented a rise of anti-Semitism on the Right. Michelle Goldberg of *Slate* thinks that having Horowitz write the piece is a shield designed to disguise *Breitbart*'s true anti-Semitic leanings. She writes, "Really, though, what *Breitbart* is doing here is playing a double game, covering anti-Semitism with a tacky sheen of philo-Semitism."[27] It should be noted, however, that *Breitbart*'s founder, the late Andrew Breitbart, was also Jewish. Moreover, *Breitbart* did cover Kristol's response on CNN fairly.[28]

According to their critics, neoconservatives are accused of not just influencing the government and the political parties and candidates. They are also said to be manipulating the media and the academy to distort the picture of

Israel's problems and provide the public a false narrative. Walt and Mearsheimer say that the website, "Campus Watch," was set up by Martin Kramer and Daniel Pipes, "two passionately pro-Israel neo-conservatives," that "posted dossiers on suspect academics and encouraged students to report remarks or behavior that might be considered hostile to Israel." Walt and Mearsheimer add, "This transparent attempt to blacklist and intimidate scholars provoked a harsh reaction and Pipes and Kramer later removed the dossiers, but the website still invites students to report 'anti-Israel' activity."[29] What Walt and Mearsheimer do not say, however, is that there is considerable blatant dishonesty about Israel in some sectors of the media and the academy. Kramer and Pipes intend only to expose just those that delegitimize and demonize Israel using lies, not any and all criticism of Israel's policies.

In reviewing Mohammad Indrees Ahmad's *The Road to Iraq: The Making of a Neoconservative War*, Robin Yassin-Kassab writes that, "The neoconservative worldview is characterized by militarism, unilateralism and a firm commitment to Zionism."[30] There are countless more statements of that kind in both the print media and in the blogosphere. A simple Google search will show the extent to which neoconservatism and Zionism are considered linked in the public's eye. A search containing the words "neoconservatism" and "Zionism" turns up over 173,000 hits. Many of these are ardent anti-Semitic websites alleging Jewish control of the U.S. government. Pat Buchanan has also routinely referred to neoconservatives as "militant Zionists."[31] The Reverend Jesse Jackson caused a minor problem for then-Senator Barack Obama when he said the presidential candidate would rid the "Zionists who have controlled American policy for decades."[32] Congressman James Traficant of Ohio said this to Greta Van Susteren on FOX News:

> Israel has a powerful stranglehold on American government. They control both members of the House and the Senate. They have us involved in wars in which we have little or no interest. Our children are coming back in body bags. The nation is bankrupt over these wars. If you open your mouth you get targeted. If they don't beat you at the poll, they'll put you in prison.[33]

Buchanan also often decries what he calls the U.S. government's post–World War II "obsession" with having more Jewish influence over America's foreign policy, citing the neoconservatives as one of many manifestations of this supposed desire to bring more Jewish representation into the State and Defense departments.[34]

However, the fact of the matter is that the neoconservatives are not Zionists. To link the two is to misunderstand both neoconservatism and Zionism. The latter is characterized by strongly nationalistic impulses that the neoconservatives actually do not have. Of the founding generation of neoconservatives, only Nathan Glazer has ever been a Zionist of any kind, and it was at a young age when he was, for a short period of time, involved in the Labor Zionist movement. Although the word "Zionist" is often used interchangeably with "pro-Israel," there is a significant difference between the two. One can be strongly supportive of Israel without being a Zionist.

Israel's critics fling around the word, "Zionism," very loosely. By Israel's supporters, the term means national pride in the Jewish people, the legitimation of the Jewish state, and a belief that Israel has the same right to defend itself against its attackers as any other country. By Israel's Jewish critics, the word is usually either used to describe an ideology that is antithetical to Judaism, or as a sacred idea that is supposed to unify the Jewish nation around Jewish values but has only been hijacked by a sinister political Right. In *The Crisis of Zionism*, Peter Beinart asserts proudly numerous times, "My grandmother made me a Zionist." However, he deplores what the movement has become.[35] On the far more bitterly hostile end are Norman Finklestein,[36] Naomi Klein, and Noam Chomsky, as well as the Neturei Karta movement of anti-Israel Haredi Jews. Gentile opponents of Israel also very often use the word. On anti-Semitic websites and social media channels, the word is ubiquitous. But even among the more moderate critics of Israel, the project of supporting Israel is very commonly put under the banner of "Zionism." In their defense, it is also probably true that people who are strongly pro-Israel also use the term to describe themselves, but their usage of the word does not make it accurate.

So what really is Zionism? It is not an ordinary kind of nationalism. What makes Zionism different is that it must necessarily begin without the unifying features that other nationalisms possess, such as a land, a language, and a way of life. When thinkers and activists first espoused Zionism in the nineteenth century, these things did not exist. Yes, there were Jews living in Palestine, but the vast majority of the world's Jewry had no recent connection to that land. Yes, there is Hebrew, but the overwhelming majority of the world's Jewry does not speak it. And yes, Judaism is as much a way of life as it is a religion, but traditions and customs are extremely diverse. Many Jews are doctrinally orthodox; others eschew the deeper currents of Judaism altogether. There are many *minhagim*, or practices, even within the Ashkenazic, Sephardic, and Oriental ethnic groups. Since this is all the case, Zionism comes in many different forms. The only unifying principle is that the Jewish people are a distinct nation and that they must have a state of their own. Following from that singular mission is the imperative need for Israelis to learn every skill and trade required for national independence, including combat, farming, and construction. While these are the universal elements of Zionism, the purpose and destiny of this Jewish state are conceived in myriads of different ways by Zionism's many varieties.

From its very beginning, Zionism was in fact a highly tendentious issue within Jewish communities. Prior to the Holocaust only a very small minority of Jews believed in it. The rabbis considered it antithetical to Judaism, and the secular leaders sought to answer the "Jewish Question" by looking for ways to assimilate into European cultures but still preserve some semblance of Jewish identity. As Gershom Scholem explains, Zionists deemed assimilation as an attempt to tell a fiction about Jewry's historic and cultural compatibility with mass gentile society. Scholem said:

> Zionism broke with all this and sought to replace fictions and games of hide-and-seek in Jewish life with honest and open relationships. It was—if I may for once avail myself of a fashionable term—an avant-garde movement, borne by a small minority that was bound to provoke the opposition of the Jewish communities precisely because of its contempt for the fictitious element in the latter's conventions."[37]

In a lecture at the University of Chicago, Leo Strauss said that it is an "undeniable fact that political Zionism, pure and simple, is based on a radical break with the principles of Jewish tradition." While Strauss was a supporter of the Zionist cause, he noted that it was a departure from Jewish prophecy that the Jewish people will one day be returned to Israel when God sends His Messiah. Although there are pacifists who separate Judaism from Zionism on the grounds that Judaism considers violence a sin, that is actually not what makes Zionism difficult to square with the precepts of Torah. It is, rather, the fact that the return from exile is supposed to happen by God's will, not by the actions of mortal men. As Strauss said in that lecture:

> Political Zionism was more passionately and more soberly concerned with the human dignity of the Jews than any other movement. What it had in mind ultimately was that the Jews should return to their land with their heads up, but not by virtue of a divine act but rather of political and military action—fighting.[38]

The Neturei Karta, a Haredi sect that opposes the existence of the modern state of Israel, writes: "In their two thousand years of Divinely decreed exile no Jew ever sought to end this exile and establish independent political sovereignty anywhere. The people's sole purpose was the study and fulfillment of the Divine commandments of the Torah."[39] There is also the Satmar Hasids, whose Rebbe calls Israeli prime ministers the "head of the heretics."[40] But these anti-Zionist leanings are confined to a minority of Haredi Jewry. Many sects of Hasidism recognize Zionism as a necessary means of securing the Jewish people's survival so that Jews can exist to study and fulfill the Divine commandments of Torah. Given the fact that anti-Semitism has throughout history threatened the safety of Jews and their religious liberty, it has come time for Jews to safeguard these things for themselves. Most also see the will of God as playing out by way of man's acts. It is akin to the

Jewish joke about the man who prays to God that he should win the lottery. Upon cursing God for not making this happen for him, God replies: "You can at least meet me halfway and buy a ticket!"

But regardless of whether one supports Zionism or not, the fact remains that Zionism cannot be equated with any other nation's patriotism because inasmuch as it seeks to preserve an ancestral past, it also solicits something new and untried. The ambition of a Zionist, secular or religious, is to establish an entirely new framework for a nation's existence for the sake of preserving an ancient heritage in some way. And, most importantly, it is not concerned with the universal rights of man. Although the Israeli Declaration of Independence notes that it will be "a country for all of its inhabitants," based on "freedom, justice, and peace," Zionism is not predicated on the natural rights of man. Nowhere in the writings and speeches of the most influential Zionist leaders, including Vladimir Jabotinsky, Moses Hess, or Theodor Herzl, is there emphasis on these modern western values. The Declaration attributes modern Israel's values to those "as envisaged to the prophets of Israel." While Israel is intended as a state devoted to western values, Zionism primarily seeks to confront the statelessness of a single nation that has been an outsider in every other society for thousands of years. As Arthur Hertzberg puts it, "The very name of the movement evoked the dream of an end of days, of an ultimate release from the exile and a coming to rest in the land of Jewry's heroic age."[41]

Because it seeks to implant the beauty of the Jewish past into the freshness of the Jewish future, Zionism has been criticized for its illiberality. A religion that was once judged as being a "fossil of history" by Sir Arnold Toynbee is now criticized for its exclusivity. Progressives today oppose nationalism, believing it to be the cause of human division. In an age when western thinking is dominated by progressive assumptions, many deem Zionism a danger to perpetual peace, and perhaps even the single greatest threat, for its focus on the good of a single nation rather than all of humanity. Asher Small, the Canadian scholar who founded and directs the Institute for the Study of Global Anti-Semitism and Policy, has said, "In the modern reinvention of the idea [of anti-Semitism] . . . it is not the Jewish people but the Jewish state that is the core problem in the world, the key obstacle to betterment."[42]

In the *New York Times*, Omri Boehm, a professor at the New School for Social Research, has argued that non-Israeli Jews also suffer from the division caused by Zionism. Boehm says that by perpetuating a narrative that Israel is the Jewish state, gentiles in every other country see their native Jewish citizens as being outsiders. For Boehm, even conservatives such as some among the "alt-right," who are supportive of Israel's right of self-determination may also have anti-Semitic feelings about their own Jewish countrymen. Boehm writes, "The idea that Israel is the Jews' own ethnic state implies that Jews living outside of it—say, in America or in Europe—enjoy a merely diasporic existence. That is another way of saying that they inhabit a country that is not genuinely their own."[43] For Boehm, the politics of Zionism are antithetical to Zionism's mandate to safeguard the rights and lives of the Jewish people in the aftermath of the Holocaust, and creates more Jewish hatred than it prevents. Although Boehm does not speak to it directly and indeed focuses his criticism on the "alt-right" and the "age of Trump," Boehm's thesis sheds light on the cause of the assumption that American Jews are motivated only by their concern for Israel rather than U.S. interests. If Jews are perceived, as having a state of their own that is not the United States, their political motivations are therefore assumed to be non-American.

While the Holocaust is regularly understood as the main catalyst igniting the popularity of Zionism, it goes further back than that. Events of anti-Semitism in Europe during the nineteenth century, such as the Dreyfus Affair in France, aroused members of the Jewish intelligentsia to form a political movement involving the establishment of a Jewish state. One of the first of these was Moses Hess, who rather than seeking equal rights for Jews in European societies as Leo Pinsker had before him sought, argued in his book, *Rome and Jerusalem*, that Jews need to create their own national state. A student of Hegel's and a friend of Karl Marx, Hess believed in a worker-led Jewish state. Hess's ideas would be a forerunner to the Labor Zionist movement. Another in the early twentieth century was Theodor Herzl, whose 1902 utopian novel, *Old New Land*, told of a socialist cooperative of Jews that would usher in a scientific and technological revolution. Herzl advocated the "Uganda Plan," which would have placed the Jewish state in central Africa.

Vladimir Jabotinsky, a "revisionist" Zionist, was a contemporary of Herzl's, but while he supported Herzl's general point about the need for Jews to found their own state, he was opposed to Herzl's socialist vision. Jabotinsky promoted the political principle of *Hadar*, which to him meant strength combined with righteousness. He believed that Jews have for centuries been moral people with clear insight on justice and morality but lacking in the strength to defend it. Zionism, to Jabotinsky, would solve that problem. For the neoconservatives, his Zionist vision is the greatest influence on the Jewish state today. In her review of Shmuel Katz's biography of Jabotinsky, Midge Decter likens his Zionist philosophy with contemporary Israeli society. She writes, "Certainly it has to be said that, in many ways, the Israelis of today answer to that description. Though they continue to live in mortal danger, unlike their ghetto forbears they also live under the protection of their brilliant yet highly potent armed forces."[44]

He was also against the "Uganda Plan" and believed that the best location for the Jewish state would be in their ancestral homeland. Although Jabotinsky was secular, he felt that the Jews must have a deep historical tie to the land they settle on. The land of Israel had been theirs until Romans, Babylonians, and later Christians conquered them. Chaim Weizmann, an erstwhile intellectual opponent of Jabotinsky's, who would later become Israel's first president, was also a supporter of that idea. One well-known anecdote that well explains why it had to be founded in Palestine was a conversation that took place between Weizmann and a member of the British House of Lords. The parliamentarian asked him, "Why do you Jews insist on Palestine when there are so many undeveloped countries you could settle in more conveniently?" Weizmann replied, "That is like my asking you why you drove twenty miles to visit your mother last Sunday when there are so many old ladies living on your street."[45]

But these are only a sample of the secular Zionist movements. Religious Zionism also arose, which envisioned the founding of the Jewish state as a literal return from exile. This form of Zionism, early led by Rabbi Zvi Hirsch Kalischer, Rabbi Moshe Shmuel Glasner, and Rabbi Abraham Isaac Kook, wanted the Jewish state to embrace the Torah commandments. The fact that Zionism comes in so many disparate varieties meant that Israel would be formed by a conflict of visions, and many of the peculiar contradictions about Israeli society that still exist today are a consequence of this conflict. On one hand, the modern state of Israel reserves a quasi-constitutional place for the rabbinate in certain social matters, such as the commissioning of marriages; but in most others, the rabbinate is secondary to the democratic legislature. There were indeed many disagreements between the religious and secular Zionists about even the most basic matters of what Israel was supposed to be. Secular Zionists won most of these conflicts of vision.

The American neoconservatives do not feel impacted by such national questions of Israeli statehood. In fact, very few non-Israeli Jews do. If the neoconservatives do feel this kind of attachment to the Zionist cause, they certainly don't speak or write about it. While Zionists are certainly very happy to have anyone's support, most of their American friends, both Jewish and gentile, are not Zionists. They may admire what the Zionists have achieved and want to help preserve it, but they are not Zionists themselves.

In fact, Charles Krauthammer has argued that by concentrating so much of the world's Jewish population into one small enclave, Zionism has made world Jewry *less* safe. In his book, *Things That Matter*, he writes:

> To destroy the Jewish people, Hitler needed to conquer the world. All that is needed today is to conquer a territory smaller than Vermont. The terrible irony is that in solving the problems of powerlessness, the Jews have necessarily put all their eggs in one basket, a small basket hard by the waters of the Mediterranean. And on its fate hinges everything Jewish.[46]

While Krauthammer acknowledges that millions of Jews live in the diaspora, assimilation and intermarriage are threatening Jewish national existence outside of Israel. In his *Weekly Standard* article, "At Last, Zion," he states: "It is my contention that on Israel—on its existence and survival—hangs the very existence and survival of the Jewish people. Or, to put the thesis in the negative, that the end of Israel means the end of the Jewish people. They survived destruction and exile at the hands of Babylon in 586 BC. They survived destruction and exile at the hands of Rome in AD 70, ad finally in AD 132. They cannot survive anther destruction and exile. The Third Commonwealth—modern Israel, born just 50 years ago—is the last."[47] Given what Krauthammer believes Jewry has to lose by the destruction of Israel, he is strongly committed to ensuring that does not happen.

But it is as American Jews that neoconservatives support the Jewish state. Norman Podhoretz reminisces in *My Love Affair With America* about having been told by Israeli Zionists that he was a bad Jew for remaining in the United States. He writes:

> No doubt the Jewish people had been in exile, but not *this* Jew, not me. My true homeland was America, and the Jewish homeland was, so far as I was concerned, a foreign country. Like England, it was a country to which I was closely related, and I was very happy that it has been established as a sovereign state to which persecuted Jews in need of refuge could flee, as millions of them, and at the cost of their lives, had been unable to do only a short while back. But I could not imagine any such thing ever happening to me, or to the Jews of America in general; and if, God forbid, it ever did and I was forced to settle in Israel, I would almost certainly feel that I was *now* in exile.[48]

Commentary magazine, it is also worth noting, has also become far less focused on Israeli and Jewish-related issues since Norman Podhoretz moved its editorial policy to the political Right. In fact, he made it focused less on Israel earlier than that, when he took control of the publication in 1960. In recent years, during Neal Kozodoy's reign as editor, it has even severed its ties altogether with the American Jewish Committee and has been publishing independently. While it is indeed true that in almost every issue there is at least one major article related to Israel or American Jewry, the magazine emphasized these topics considerably more under the direction of its founding editor, Elliot Cohen. In its early years, *Commentary* was heavily focused on analyzing the efforts of the Zionists in Israel and how they would reshape life for Jews in the diaspora. An interesting anecdote Norman recalls in *Making It* is the occasion when Cohen said to him, "The main difference between *Partisan Review* and *Commentary* is that we admit to being a Jewish magazine and they don't."[49] But when Cohen passed on and Podhoretz took the reigns, he changed the magazine's tone vis-à-vis the emphasis it places on Jewish and Zionist themes more toward the direction of concentrating on broader American political and cultural problems.

Jacob Heilbrunn in *They Knew They Were Right* contends that the first generation of neoconservatives was not even that focused on Israel until the 1960s, even though they were working at a magazine that was. Irving Kristol had been its religion editor and Podhoretz was primarily writing literary reviews, while Nathan Glazer and Midge Decter were primarily writing about domestic sociological problems. In reviewing back issues of *Commentary* from the 1950s, Heilbrunn's point is accurate. He suggests that the key factors in kindling their interest in Israel were the trial of Adolph Eichmann, the Six Day War, and black anti-Semitism in the United States.[50] There is scant evidence for the latter being much of a catalyst, but the first two are certainly key events that spawned their heavy interest in Israel.

Inasmuch as it was not an issue spawning the neoconservative ascendency out of Jewish liberalism, relations between the Jewish and African-American communities has indeed been a topic of reflection in the pages of *Commentary* over the years. The most notable is Norman Podhoretz's candid but daring essay, "My Negro Problem—And Ours," but that was in 1963 when he was still very much on the political Left. There have, however, been conflicts between the Israel lobby and African-American leaders over the years, in which *Commentary* was integral in defending the side of Israel, including the Congressional Black Caucus's 2015 support of the boycott of Benjamin Netanyahu's Iran speech before a joint session of Congress. Also, in 1995 Joshua Muravchik criticized the Congressional Black Caucus for applauding Louis Farrakahn's anti-Semitic rhetoric.[51]

Perhaps the major first example was the "Andrew Young Affair" in 1979. Young was America's United Nations ambassador who, against President Carter's policy, had held a private meeting with senior leaders of the Palestinian Liberation Organization (PLO). The official policy of the U.S. government was not to recognize the legitimacy of the PLO. The meeting therefore led to Young's resignation. Young, being the first black ambassador to the UN, was most certainly a hero to the black community, which took it as a major slight to their advancement in American society that, from his point of view, Jews were responsible for causing him to resign. Young had gone on *Face the Nation* alluding to that, when he said that remaining ambassador after his unauthorized meeting with PLO officials would "have torn up the Democratic Party,"[52] implying that the livid reaction of the influential Jewish donors suggested there would be a civil war between the Jewish and black members of the party if he did not step down. Feeling that he needed to give an oppressed group a sympathetic ear, he remarked, "I feel like I'm an innocent bystander being swept along by the forces of history."[53] Carl Gershman wrote an essay in *Commentary* following Young's CBS interview, condemning Young's assertion that what he, as the first black UN ambassador representing the United States, was being unjustly scapegoated by the Jews in his party. Gershman insisted that what Young did was endanger "democracy and its enemies . . . the same democratic commitment that led Jews and others to support the civil rights movement."[54]

Gershman also lamented that the "Andrew Young Affair" instigated a growing tide of anti-Semitism among black leaders. He feared that unless American Jews reject the paradigm that the affair had to do with black-Jewish relations, it would imperil the preservation not only of Jewry but also of all democratic values. He wrote:

> Jews will have no choice but to resist [Young's] point of view, and not just out of a commitment to Israel. The chances for Jewish survival in a world dominated by the Soviet Union and its "nonaligned" allies may not be entirely foreclosed, but survival under these conditions is not a cheerful prospect to contemplate.[55]

Years after the Andrew Young incident, neoconservatives have seen the liberal Jewish establishment as failing to heed the kind of advice Gershman gave them in his 1979 essay. Neal Kozodoy later wrote:

> As the aftermath of the Andrew Young affair made clear, some Jews seem particularly adept at dodging what a more self-respecting political culture would define as their duty, and what a liberal order guarantees as their right: the duty and the right to stand up and defend oneself when attacked.[56]

It is clear, however, that even as Podhoretz's *Commentary* had fewer articles devoted to Jewish themes, they were still very present in the magazine under Podhoretz's control, just to a much lesser extent than it had been under Cohen. As Ruth Wisse has written, "The magazine's most obvious challenge was how to balance being 'American,' 'intellectual,' 'independent, and 'Jewish.'"[57] Each of its four editors-in-chief—Cohen, Norman Podhoretz, Neal Kozodoy, and John Podhoretz—have answered that challenge in different ways.

NOTES

1. Paul Findlay, forward to Stephen J. Sniegoski, *The Transparent Cabal: The Neoconservative Agenda in the Middle East, and the National Interest of Israel* (Virginia: Enigma Editions, 2008), p. vii.
2. Ibid.
3. R. Emmett Tyrell Jr., *The Conservative Crack-Up* (New York: Simon & Schuster, 1992), p. 87.
4. John Mearsheimer and Stephen Walt, "The Israel Lobby," *London Review of Books*, Vol. 28, No. 6, March 23, 2006.
5. Michael Walzer, "Why Are Jews Liberal? (An Alternative to Norman Podhoretz)," *Dissent*, October 30, 2009.
6. Norman Podhoretz, *World War IV: The Long Struggle Against Islamo-Fascism* (New York: Doubleday, 2007) p. 61.
7. Interview with Norman Podhoretz.

8. Scott McConnell, "I Like and Respect Israel—But It's Not America," *The American Conservative*, September 26, 2012.
9. Robert Novak, "Worse Than Apartheid?" *Washington Post*, April 9, 2007.
10. Paul Craig Roberts, "Massive Defeat For US Neocon Nazis and Israel's Crazed Netanyahu," *paulcraigroberts.org*, April 2, 2015.
11. Russell Kirk, "Neoconservatism: An Endangered Species," Heritage.org (http://www.heritage.org/research/lecture/the-neoconservatives-an-endangered-species).
12. Joshua Muravchik, "Pat Buchanan and the Jews," *Commentary*, January 1991.
13. David Frum, *Dead Right* (New York: Basic Books, 1995), p. 155.
14. Ibid, p. 156.
15. William F. Buckley, *In Search of Anti-Semitism* (New York: Continuum International Publishing Group, 1992), p. 126.
16. Michael Brendan Dougherty has suggested that Sobran was not really a revisionist of the Holocaust, but traveled with such people for financial gain, following the demise of his writing career in mainstream print. See Dougherty, "I Will Miss Joe Sobran," *The American Conservative*, October 1, 2010.
17. Joseph Sobran, "For Fear of the Jews," *Sobran's* (http://www.sobran.com/fearofjews.shtml).
18. William F. Buckley, *In Search of Anti-Semitism*, p. 13.
19. Ibid, p. 9.
20. Stephen B. Smith, "Leo Strauss's Forgotten Letter," *Commentary*, September 13, 2016.
21. Joseph Sobran, "How I Was Fired By Bill Buckley," reprinted in *Voice of Reason*, October 2, 2010.
22. The Editors, "The Year That Conservatism Turned Ugly," *First Things*, May 1992.
23. Samuel Francis, *James Burnham: Thinkers of Our Time* (United Kingdom: Claridge Press, 1999), p. 118. Burnham does say also that the neoconservatives are in a "transitional state."
24. Sobran, "How I Was Fired By Bill Buckley."
25. David Horowitz, "Bill Kristol: Republican Spoiler, Renegade Jew?" *Breitbart*, May 15, 2016.
26. Ibid.
27. Michelle Goldberg, "Breitbart Calls Trump Foe 'Renegade Jew.' This is How Anti-Semitism Goes Mainstream," *Slate*, May 16, 2016.
28. *Breitbart TV*, "Kristol Responds to 'Renegade Jew' Article: 'I'm a Proud Jew, Strong Supporter of Israel," *Breitbart*, May 17, 2016.
29. John Mearsheimer and Stephen Walt, "The Israel Lobby," *London Review of Books*, March 2006.
30. Robin Yassin-Kassab, "How neoconservatives led US to war in Iraq," *The National*, December 11, 2014 (http://www.thenational.ae/arts-lifestyle/the-review/how-neoconservatives-led-us-to-war-in-iraq).
31. Pat Buchanan, "On to Damascus?," *World Net Daily*, April 9, 2003.
32. Natasha Mozgovaya, "Obama Camp Dismisses Jesse Jackson's Israel Policy Remarks," *Ha'aretz*, October 14, 2008.
33. Greta Van Susteren's interview with James Traficant, *Fox News*, September 10, 2009.
34. Pat Buchanan, *A Republic, Not an Empire* (New York: Regnery, 2002), p. 336.
35. Peter Beinart, *The Crisis of Zionism* (United Kingdom: Picador Publishing, 2013), p. 4.
36. Jordan Michael Smith, "An Unpopular Man," *The New Republic* July 7, 2015.
37. Gershom Scholem, "Israel and the Diaspora," in *On Jews and Judaism in Crisis: Selected Essays* (New York: Paul Dry Books, 2012), pp. 246–247.
38. Leo Strauss, "Why We Remain Jews," *Jewish Philosophy and the Crisis of Modernity* (New York: Study of Jewish Community Organization, 1962), p. 319.
39. Neturei Karta, "Judaism and Zionism Are Not the Same Thing," Nkusa.org (http://www.nkusa.org/AboutUs/Zionism/judaism_isnot_zionism.cfm).
40. *Arutz Sheva* Staff, "Satmar Rebbe: 'Tear Your Garment' Over Netanyahu," *Arutz Sheva*, May 22, 2018.

41. Arthur Hertzberg, *The Zionist Idea* (New York: The Jewish Publication Society, 1997), p. 16.
42. Sam Sokol, "'Institutional Anti-Semitism' Exists in the U.S., Expert Says," *Jerusalem Post*, February 19, 2015.
43. Omri Boehm, "Liberal Zionism in the Age of Trump," *New York Times*, December 20, 2016.
44. Midge Decter, "Lone Wolf: A Biography of Vladimir (Ze'ev) Jabotinsky by Shmuel Katz," *Commentary*, July 1, 1996.
45. Noah Pollack, "Weizmann's Answer," *Commentary*, October 8, 2007.
46. Charles Krauthammer, *Things That Matter* (New York: Crown Forum, 2003), p. 271.
47. Charles Krauthammer, "At Last, Zion," *The Weekly Standard*, May 11, 1998.
48. Norman Podhoretz, *My Love Affair With America: The Cautionary Tale of a Cheerful Conservative* (New York: The Free Press, 2000), p. 52.
49. Norman Podhoretz, *Making It* (New York: Random House, 1967), pp. 99–101.
50. Jacob Heilbrunn, *They Knew They Were Right* (New York: Doubleday, 2008), p. 67.
51. Joshua Muravchik, "Facing Up to Black Anti-Semitism," *Commentary*, December 1, 1995.
52. Carl Gershman, "The Andrew Young Affair," *Commentary*, November 1, 1979.
53. Ibid.
54. Ibid.
55. Ibid.
56. Benjamin Balint, *Running Commentary* (New York: Public Affairs, 2011), p. 133.
57. Ruth Wisse, "The Jewishness of *Commentary*," in *Commentary in American Life*, ed. Murray Friedman (Philadelphia, PA: Temple University Press), p. 55.

Chapter Two

More Concern for Israel's Interests Than America's?

Contrary to what many of Israel's critics say, the vast majority of Jews, neoconservatives included, do not take every criticism of Israel as anti-Semitic. Nathan Glazer acknowledges this point and the problem critics of Israel have of walking a tight rope between legitimate criticism of Israel and anti-Semitism. He writes:

> The key problem in isolating the evil of anti-Semitism in American political controversy in the 1990's is complicated because there is a Jewish state, a major actor in a very important part of the world. When one adds that a strong lobby defends Israel's interests, that politicians must often walk on eggshells when they talk about Israel and that they sometimes take positions they personally disagree with because of the strength of the lobby and the passion of Jewish contributors, the difficulty becomes clear. All these are or should be legitimate issues in political discourse. But how do those who believe the nation would be better off if it were less committed to Israel and more friendly toward Israel's enemies (in whose lands oil is abundant) avoid the accusation of anti-Semitism?[1]

The Israeli politician, Natan Sharansky, has posited what he calls the "3-D Test" of whether an idea is anti-Semitic in regards to Israel. He suggests that an idea is anti-Semitic if it "demonizes" or "delegitimizes" Israel or holds the Jewish state to a "double standard." Sharansky introduced this test in the *Forward* in 2005. He says, "This "3-D" test applies the same criteria to the new antisemitism that for centuries identified different manifestations of classical antisemitism."[2] And while not every criticism of the Israel lobby is anti-Semitic either, the same test could apply to whether or not opposition to them crosses over into the realm of anti-Semitism. However, since this is an

American lobby rather than the Israeli state itself, it is also necessary to add a fourth D to the test: "disloyalty." It crosses into anti-Semitic terrain when the supporters of Israel are branded as subversives who are only interested in the interests of another country, as Gore Vidal, for example, branded the Podhoretzes in the 1980s. In an article he published in *The Nation* titled, "The Empire Strikes Back," Vidal wrote: "[Norman] and Midge stay on among us in order to make propaganda and raise money for Israel—a country they don't seem eager to live in."[3]

As for Sharansky's Ds and how they apply to attitudes about members of the Israel lobby, there are several standard positions espoused by their critics. They are demonized when they are compared with Nazis and accused of being warmongering bigots who just want to see Muslims exterminated. They are delegitimized when the country they want America to support is seen as an occupier rather than a legitimate sovereign state. And they are held to a "double standard" when their lobby is singled out as the only cohesive task force with power and influence in government, the press, and the academy.

Not every criticism of the neoconservatism amounts to these four "D" criteria. In fact, most do not. There are plenty of grounds to criticize neoconservatives for making calculations that do not come true, for destabilizing the Middle East, for putting too much faith in the peace potential of democracy, and for thinking of Israel as sharing all of the same interests of the United States. Policies of isolationism, offshore balancing, or liberal internationalism may very well be more rational models for the United States on many given issues. It is easy to see when a criticism of neoconservatives is not anti-Semitic when the inclusion of other lobbies, movements, and perspectives are added to those being criticized. And when respect is at least given to the neoconservatives' intellectual credentials and for their good intentions, no one is interpreting anti-Semitism as the underlying subtext. But there are, indeed, critics who seem single-mindedly obsessed with the neoconservatives who consider them to have illicit ambitions and disproportionate influence over America's policymakers and public opinion.

Critics of neoconservatives often cite a 1996 policy brief put out by the Institute for Advanced Strategic and Policy Studies, an Israeli think tank, titled, "A Clean Break: A New Strategy for Securing the Realm." The paper, allegedly authored by a group led by Richard Perle and Douglas Feith, is said to have been a primer for Benjamin Netanyahu's first term as prime minister of the Knesset. The paper lists the "rebuilding of Zionism" as one of Likud's main goals. According to the document, denationalizing Israel's economy is the starting point of this objective, but so is "forging a new basis of relations with the U.S," including relying less on American economic aid and creating more cooperative defense programs between the two countries.[4] Citations of this document thusly described are found in writings by Buchanan, Sniegorski, and throughout the Internet. However, Perle and Feith did not author the "Clean Break" paper. Its rapporteur was David Wurmster, who during the Bush years was an aide to Vice President Dick Cheney and UN Ambassador John Bolton. Wurmster produced it as manifesto of his own thoughts on Israeli-American relations and Israeli economic reform was indeed its main focus. He invited a number of prominent neoconservative figures to discuss his points at a seminar in Israel and the list of names on the document were those people. Critics misconstrue them as signatories. They did not endorse it, but rather were on the guest list that was asked by Wurmster to read it prior to their attendance. Perle and Feith did not even attend.[5] Feith stated, "In fact, my relationship to the paper is like that of an individual mentioned on a book's acknowledgement page—simply someone with whom the author consulted in the course of his work. It would be foolish to describe all the names on a book's acknowledgement page as co-authors. And it is foolish to describe me as co-author of the 'Clean Break' paper."[6] In 2004, the *Washington Post* issued a clarification about its previous reporting of the document, stating these facts and adding: "The report was not commissioned by Mr. Netanyahu."[7]

It is also purported that President Clinton received a letter signed by several neoconservatives, including Perle, William Kristol, Elliot Abrams, Robert Kagan, Paul Wolfowitz, William Bennett, and Donald Rumsfeld, urging him to endorse the brief's objectives in his State of the Union Address. However, their letter to Clinton did not cite the "Clean Break" paper or its points. It is certainly true that these individuals were long advocating regime change in Iraq throughout the 1990s, but not necessarily for the sake of Israeli interests. *Washington Times* editor-at-large, Arnaud de Borchgrave, has also alleged that Ariel Sharon and George W. Bush, whose administration was staffed by many Jewish neoconservative policy advisors, later aligned for "Judeo-Christian" interests to work toward the goals enumerated in the document, including regime change in Iraq. Borchgrave writes, "Washington's 'Likudniks,' Ariel Sharon's powerful backers in the Bush administration have been in charge of U.S. policy in the Middle East since President Bush was sworn into office."[8] In *Where the Right Went Wrong*, Pat Buchanan cites Borchgrave's column as an exposure of the Republican Party's neoconservative stronghold.[9]

There is, of course, also the allegation that neoconservatives are warmongering just for its own sake, and that it is not so much a love for Israel that drives them but rather a deep hatred of Muslims. Fred Kaplan of *Slate*, for instance, went so far as to accuse the neoconservatives, Israel, and King Salman of Saudi Arabia of opposing President Obama's 2015 agreement with Iran because it takes war off the table. Even as Kaplan himself admits that there are substantive problems with the Iran deal, he authors a column glossing over them and accusing its neoconservative detractors of treachery.

Kaplan writes, "Their view is the opposite of Winston Churchill's: They believe to war-war is better than to jaw-jaw."[10] While Kaplan's case about King Salman has merit because there is indeed a Sunni hatred of Shiites and seeing Israel and the United States kill them would serve his aims, what the neoconservatives and Israel stand to gain by war for its own sake Kaplan does not say.

Stephen Walt and John Mearsheimer argue that the "loose coalition" they call the "Israel Lobby," comprised largely of neoconservatives, is more concerned about Israeli interests than American. These two political scientists are devotees of the "realist" paradigm of international relations theory. Countering the Wilsonian "idealist" school, which says that states can form alliances around common values, "realism" purports that states enter into alliances that maximize their own national interest, unless domestic politics interferes. For Walt and Mearsheimer, America's national interest is actually served by being less allied with Israel. Arab nations that are deemed enemies are oil-rich, whereas Israel has no oil, other than the most recent natural gas discovery, which occurred long after Mearsheimer and Walt published their book. Moreover, they say that Israel is a "strategic burden." "Backing Israel was not cheap," they say, "and it complicated America's relations with the Arab world."[11] As realist political scientists, they seek to explain the America's pro-Israel foreign policy in light of the economic and tactical costs, which they insist are not worth the benefits. For them, it is the domestic interference of the neoconservatives and others in the powerful Israel Lobby that influence policymakers to ally the United States with a country that is antithetical to American interests. Walt and Mearsheimer are assuming that the neoconservatives agree with them that the two countries' interests do not align but want to give priority to Israel anyway. It will be demonstrated here later that this is not the neoconservatives' point of view. In fact, neoconservatives see the two countries' as being natural allies because they see the interests of both countries as coinciding.

There is also the simple fact that Israel actually opposed the Iraq War. It was actually Iran that Ariel Sharon and other Israeli leaders wanted the United States to attack. Israel had not been very worried about Iraq's nuclear program since they destroyed the Osirak reactor in 1981. According to Lawrence Wilkerson, a State Department official under Colin Powell, "The Israelis were telling us Iraq is not the enemy—Iran is the enemy."[12] Israel had not considered Iraq a direct threat since the 1980s. Its own intelligence on Iraq's weapons capabilities revealed that it had not had the long-range missiles to deliver either conventional or biological bombs into Israel. It was the Americans and British that had different intelligence. Israel's leaders were publicly silent on the issue during the early days of the war, but Ambassador Danny Ayalon later revealed that he was instructed by Prime Minister Sharon not to recommend war on Iraq to the United States. He also stated that Sharon himself advised President Bush that invading Iraq without an exit strategy would greatly destabilize the region, which would be against Israel's own interests. Ayalon also states that he remembers Sharon telling Bush, "In terms of culture and tradition, the Arab world is not built for democratization."[13]

Saddam's Ba'ath regime was also not as much of a funder of Palestinian terrorism as Iran and other Arab countries, which Israel likewise knew. The most significant exception was Saddam's support of the Arab Liberation Front, a group within the PLO, which primarily helped in the form of financial aid for the families of suicide bombers.[14] Palestinians considered Saddam Hussein a hero, indeed, but not enough of a thorn in Israel's backside for them to urge the United States to take him out. It is indeed true that neoconservatives were still motivated anyway by Israel's security concerns when they pushed for the invasion of Iraq, fearing that Saddam would use weapons of mass destruction against Israel. They did disagree with Brent Scowcroft's concern that an invasion would spearhead Iraq's retaliation against Israel with WMD's and that America should be focused instead on securing peace between Israel and the Palestinians to quell the anti-Israel fervor in the region.[15] They believed that Israel's safety necessitates regime change in Iraq before they have the chance to use them and that the Israeli-Palestinian conflict is a tangential matter at best. However, Israel's security was more of a tertiary motivation for their call for an invasion, as indicated by many of their writings. As John Podhoretz said, "Those who supported the war, in overwhelming numbers, believed there were multiple justifications for it."[16] And most importantly, neoconservatives did not advocate invasion at the behest of the Israeli government.

Nor is it true that the neoconservatives will always necessarily side with Israel in any disagreement between the two countries. For example, when Jonathan Pollard was still incarcerated for espionage against the United States and Israelis were passionately hoping for his release from U.S. federal prison, not all neoconservatives joined the "Justice for Pollard" movement or agreed with Netanyahu's plea for his release. Charles Krauthammer, for example, disappointed Israelis when he said: "I have never had any sympathy for Pollard. I'm not talking about the justice of the sentence, or the lightness or seriousness of it, I'm just talking about the action Pollard took himself, and I think it's something for which I have absolutely no sympathy."[17]

Another notable instance was in 1992 after President George H.W. Bush and Secretary of State James Baker delayed loan guarantees to Israel for its absorption of Russian Jewish refugees. The Bush administration felt that Prime Minister Yitzhak Shamir's continued settlement construction was as an obstacle to peace in the region. While the American Israel Public Affairs Committee (AIPAC) was angered over Bush's decision, there was not a uniform neoconservative reaction. In fact, *Commentary* held a debate on this matter in its October issue, between Daniel Pipes and Martin Peretz. Pipes argued that the loan guarantee "imbroglio" was an inconsequential issue, given how much financial aid Washington has already been providing Israel, and because in this case Bush was only delaying the loan guarantees, not withholding them outright. Pipes also said that, if anything, Bush's decision was good for Israel because it would encourage more economic independence from the United States. Pipes said: "Doing *without* the loan guarantee probably would have served Israel's long-term interests. To absorb immigrants, the country needs growth, not aid. Yet by permitting Israeli politicians to defer the hard decisions, American handouts permit Israel's dinosaur socialist institutions to limp along. The prospect of no loan guarantee compelled the Israeli government to get serious about economic reforms, privatization in particular."[18]

The best example, however, is the Egyptian uprising in 2011. The neoconservatives supported the protests and were happy to see the tyrannical reign of Hosni Mubarek come to an end. Although they watched with skeptical eyes, their overall position was that progress could be fomenting toward a new democratic Egypt. Israel, on the other hand, was frightened by the developments in Cairo. Mubarek was a tyrant, but he was a tyrant who kept the thirty-year peace between the two countries, resorting to force over his own citizens in order to maintain it. Elliot Abrams said this to Jeffrey Goldberg of *The Atlantic*:

> The Israelis first of all do not believe in the universality of democracy. They believe Arab culture does not permit democracy. They see a danger in Mubarak's fall, and they are right: we do not know who will take over now or in a year or two from now. But this is at bottom a crazy reaction. What they are afraid of is the Muslim Brotherhood, right? Mubarak has ruled for THIRTY YEARS and leaves us a Brotherhood that is that powerful? Isn't that all the proof we need that dictatorship is not the way to fight the Brotherhood? He crushed the moderate and centrist groups and left the Brothers with an open field. He is to blame for the Brothers' popularity and strength right now. The sooner he goes the better.[19]

But Benjamin Netanyahu predicted that the January 25 Revolution would lead Egypt to becoming another Iran. He said this to German chancellor Angela Merkel:

> Our real fear is of a situation that could develop . . . and which has already developed in several countries including Iran itself—repressive regimes of radical Islam. . . . In a situation of chaos, an organized Islamist body can seize control of a country. It happened in Iran. It happened in other instances.[20]

While neoconservatives agree with Israel's Likud on the vast majority of geopolitical issues, the two have been at odds over what the Arab Spring promises for the region, and this is not a trivial difference of opinion. As Shmuel Rosner said: "The Egyptian unrest provides a great opportunity to refute once and for all the ridiculous but still strangely common belief that Israelis or, even more commonly, 'Likudniks' are the oriental equivalent of American neocons."[21] It also refutes once and for all the premise that neoconservatives look at everything from the lens of what is best for Israel. Their actual scope takes in a much larger picture of the globe.

It is also important to note that neoconservatism actually has origins in the realist paradigm. Irving Kristol, the "grandfather of neoconservatism," was a realist who aligned with many of the Cold War views of Hans J. Morgenthau and Henry Kissinger. He and Owen Harries co-founded *The National Interest* not to advance Wilsonian global idealism but as a journal of international realism. The magazine today, although sometimes confused for being a neoconservative publication, is actually quite critical of neoconservatives from the realist perspective. In fact, even the "About" section of *The National Interest*'s website accuses "liberal hawks and neoconservatives" of "having successfully attempted to stifle debate."[22] The very publication that Kristol co-founded has joined in the anti-neocon chorus.

Norman Podhoretz, on the other hand, never considered himself of the realist school. At one time, he thought of himself as a "hard Wilsonian" as opposed to a "soft Wilsonian." He has, however, backtracked from that, citing Charles Kesler's book, *I am the Change: Barack Obama and the Crisis of Liberalism*, as having influenced his thinking about the compatibility of his views with Woodrow Wilson's.[23] But his model of foreign policy lacks agreement with some of the most definitive realist premises, most especially the notion of balance of power. However, his paradigm resembles some other aspects of realism, such as believing in the need for vast military strength to promote U.S. interests. The only difference is that far more than realists do, Podhoretz believes it is imperative to national interests for the United States to be in control of as many situations that arise in the world as it can. This is in contrast to realism, which maintains that the purpose of the vast arsenal is to deter attacks on America and her allies or to go war to restore power balances. Irving Kristol, in his usual skeptical way, never fully embraced this new approach, but was later moved to support it in light of what he saw as failures of realism to adequately contain communism.[24]

What this means for the neoconservative defense of Israel is that they have always seen the Jewish state as a vital ally in the American effort to control world events. They maintained this during and after the Cold War. And while there were realists during the Cold War who did not share their view, some did, most especially Henry Kissinger. Even President Nixon, hardly a neoconservative or a philo-Semite, saw the catastrophic effects Israel's obliteration would have had on America's Cold War interests. That is why he ordered the airlift during the Yom Kippur War to reinforce supplies to Israel at the behest of Golda Meir. Losing Israel would have completely ceded the Middle East to the Soviets, who were strongly backing Israel's Arab enemies. It is true that helping Israel risked losing the Arab oil supply, but given that the United States has far more energy independence than Europe and also gets a bulk of its oil from Latin America—a region the United States has more control over than the Middle East—it seemed to Nixon to be a fair calculation in his costs/benefits analysis that this was the right decision. Nixon would later write in his book, *1999: Victory Without War*, "Our commitment to the survival of Israel runs deep. We are not formal allies, but we are bound together by something much stronger than any piece of paper: a moral commitment. It is a commitment which no President in the past has ever broken and which every future President will faithfully honor. America will never allow the sworn enemies of Israel to achieve their goal of destroying it."[25]

Neoconservatives believe that the United States is in a unique position of having far more options at its disposal than other countries have. While France was at one time one of Israel's strongest allies and weapons providers, it and the rest of Europe refused to help Israel in this existential crisis because their options were a lot more limited. It is not that Europe wanted to see Israel obliterated, but they had succumbed to Soviet pressure in a way that the United States was not threatened with. Joshua Muravchik notes in his book, *The Imperative of American Leadership* that Kissinger and Nixon considered Europe's refusal to even allow the United States to land there for refueling to be a violation of the NATO agreement.[26] But as Muravchik argues, alliances do not solve every problem and that America has to often act alone to lead the world. And while liberal internationalists prefer the apparatus of the United Nations in addressing problems like the Israeli-Palestinian conflict, neoconservatives argue that it is an especially corrupt and failed device, with the decks unreasonably stacked Israel in the General Assembly. For example, in 2015, there were six General Assembly resolutions passed condemning Israel and none condemning China, Cuba, Saudi Arabia, Syria, Venezuela, or ISIS.[27]

Paleoconservatives like Buchanan who loathe America's involvement in the United Nations should realize that they have a friend in the neoconservatives on that point. Perhaps for different reasons, both movements see the UN as an obstacle to American interests. There could be some rapprochement between the two of them on this issue that they fail to exploit. Inasmuch as their foreign policies differ with regards to isolation versus intervention, both wings of conservatism think the UN causes far more trouble in the world than it solves. Particularly on the matter of Israel, neoconservatives believe the UN creates political and emotional entanglements between its member countries that add too many extraneous, tangential considerations for the actual actors in the conflict, making it that much more difficult for concessions to be reached. As Irving Kristol put it, "The situation in the Middle East would be much less explosive than it is, and negotiations among interested parties would be more serious than they are, did the UN not exist." Kristol adds: "All parties with authentic, material interests in the Israeli-Arab conflict would have more 'space' for maneuver, did not the UN create a spurious 'world opinion' that constricts such flexibility."[28] In a panel discussion at the Heritage Foundation, Midge Decter said that the UN has become "a center for the articulation and the legitimization of tyranny, in the names of 'justice,' 'freedom,' and all those other words which we contributed and which daily get perverted."[29]

One of their concerns regarding Israel has been making sure a repeat of past disasters does not happen. On too many occasions bad outcomes have come to Israel after the United States cautioned the Israelis to restrain themselves. For example, in 1967 after Israel took control of the Sinai Peninsula, President Johnson assured Israel that they would "use all and every measures" to open the Straits of Tiran and the Suez Canal, urging Israel not to take action. When it turned out that Johnson's "every measure" promise ran as far as merely putting economic pressure on Abdul Nasser, Prime Minister Levi Eshkol was left in the lurch. He informed the president that Israel was "approaching a point at which counsels of restraint would lack any moral or logical basis" and that Israel was "experiencing some of the heaviest days in its history."[30]

Another example was Nixon and Kissinger's recommendation to Golda Meir in 1973 against a preemptive strike, despite advanced warnings of a looming Egyptian-Syrian attack. Norman Podhoretz was also livid that in 1981, President Reagan instructed fellow neoconservative, Ambassador Jeanne Kirkpatrick, to vote yes on a UN Security Council resolution condemning Israel for unilaterally taking out Iraq's Osirak reactor, and then for three months suspended arms transfers to Israel.[31] There was also much neoconservative fury directed at President George W. Bush when in 2002 he ordered Ariel Sharon to withdraw from Operation Defensive Shield. All of these American decisions frustrated neoconservatives, especially considering that two of them came from presidents they thought they could trust to stand by Israel. They have ever since maintained a "never again" attitude about judgment mistakes in America's relations with Israel.

Neoconservatives also part ways with the realists by conceiving of the national interest ideationally. They believe in a moral global order and see America as necessarily being the hegemonic leader in safeguarding human rights across the world. They see America's honor as being just as important to the national interests as economic prosperity and homeland security. In a 1996 *Commentary* article titled, "American Power—A Guide for the Perplexed," Robert Kagan writes: "How did we arrive at the perception that our national interest is something clear and calculable, involving only such tangible and measurable things as oil reserves and military bases, and excluding such intangibles as principles, ideas, or 'American values'"? And Kagan argues that the realist perspective of the national interest is a newer, late-twentieth-century attitude, not the opinion of America's founders. He adds: "As it happens, today's common definition is neither self-evident nor eternal nor even 'traditional.' If someone had asked Alexander Hamilton what the national interest was, he would have alluded to prosperity and security from foreign influence, but he would have also invoked the need to lift his young country into a place of honor among the world's great powers."[32]

If helping the Jewish state survive is the right thing to do, the neoconservatives believe the United States must do it for the sake of America's honor. But if democratization of the Arab world is also the right thing to do and ultimately create for a more peaceful, stable world, America must promote that even if Israel perceives it to be against its short-term or even long-term interests. Thus, Israel as well as Europe must also be led by the United States, according to the neoconservatives.

However, during the years of the Obama presidency the neoconservatives regarded Israel—particularly its leader, Netanyahu—as taking the moral high road over the United States on the Iran agreement. Ruth Wisse stated that Netanyahu's speech before Congress in 2015 should have "been given by the commander-in-chief of the world's superpower rather than by the leader of the Jewish state, if only because sooner or later American strength will be required to defeat the new super-threats." She also invoked the Talmudic proverb in her praise of Netanyahu: "In a place where there are no men, strive to be a man."[33] *Commentary*'s Jonathan Tobin lamented the "deafening silence" at the UN when Netanyahu spoke in 2015 to a smaller audience of delegations, telling them, "That Iran is still set on opposing U.S. interests, spreading terror and working toward regional hegemony, topics that the president conspicuously avoided in his speech."[34]

It is not that neoconservatives glorify Netanyahu or Israel but rather that they are frustrated that the U.S. president does not have the same good sense that they think Bibi has. To them, Netanyahu was the only courageous world leader, fighting for the survival of the West even while Western leaders would not heed his words. Israel, they believe, has been the most rational actor on the Iranian nuclear crisis, while it has been Obama and European leaders who are wedded to the belief that the Iranians can be bargained with diplomatically. Realists, meanwhile, either support Iran's nuclear proliferation as having a positive balancing effect in the region—as in the case of Kenneth Waltz[35]—or view America's best option to be working to negotiate a peace deal between the Israelis and Palestinians. Neoconservatives believe that both of those views are absurd. To Waltz's argument, you do not allow an irrational tyrant access to nuclear weapons, and to the latter, Israel's conflict with the Palestinians is just a red herring played up by the Arab world to vilify Israel. As Iranian journalist Amir Taheri puts it in *Commentary*: "Far from being the root cause of instability and war in the wider Middle East, one could argue that the Israeli-Palestinian conflict is rather peripheral, and that the region's deeper and much more intractable problems lie elsewhere. And one would be right."[36]

The neoconservatives were not just thinking about Israel's survival, although it was clearly one of their main concerns. They were not absolutely confident that Iran would actually use its nuclear capabilities against Israel, as there are both strategic and religious reasons why Iran would not do it at this point in time, but the feasibility still cannot be counted out and certainly long-run possibilities have to be considered. But to the neoconservatives, the Iran agreement would have more far-reaching dire consequences than that. Looked at from the realist perspective, it would dramatically alter the balance of power in the region, negating Israel's upper hand, which the United States vitally depends on. They also agreed with the realists George Schultz and Henry Kissinger that the American objective must always remain to be the prevention of nuclear proliferation in Iran rather than curbing it down. An agreement that allows Iran to develop nuclear capabilities for non-aggressive use would create "huge inspections problems," Kissinger said. But the worst-case scenario that Rick Richman cites in *Commentary* is Kissinger's argument before the Senate Armed Services Committee: "If the other countries in the region conclude that America has approved the development of an enrichment capability within one year of a nuclear weapon, and if they then insist on building the same capability, we will live in a proliferated world."[37]

Neoconservatives live by the rule that the United States should never look weak. They believe America cannot lead if respect for its vast power is lost. We have to mean what we say and say what we mean. The United States can be open to compromise but only if the upper hand rests with America in all bargaining situations. And the United States will be taken seriously, they argue, if it is only prepared to use its military in narrow pinprick exercises that do nothing but create short-term hiccups. During the 1990s the neoconservatives devoted a lot of time to trying to convince President Clinton to "take the difficult but inescapable net step of finishing the job [George H. W.] Bush started," as Bill Kristol and Kagan put it.[38] They now likewise believe it is folly to allow the Iran government to proliferate weapons of mass destruction, especially after several Iranian leaders have called Israel's annihilation "non-negotiable."[39]

NOTES

1. Nathan Glazer, "The Enmity Within," *New York Times Book Review*, September 27, 1992.
2. Natan Sharansky, "Antisemitism in 3-D," *Forward*, January 21, 2005.

Chapter 2

3. Gore Vidal, "The Empire Strikes Back," *The Nation*, March 22, 1986.
4. Although the paper does not seem to be readily available, a summary of the paper can be found at http://www.informationclearinghouse.info/article1438.htm, July 10, 2018.
5. Interview with Joshua Muravchik, June 16, 2016.
6. "Feith For the Record—The 'Clean Break' Paper," *DougFeith.com*.
7. "Credit for Israel Report Clarified," *Washington Post*, September 16, 2004, p. A30.
8. Arnaud de Borchgrave, "A Bush-Sharon Doctrine?," *Washington Times*, February 14, 2003.
9. Pat Buchanan, *Where the Right Went Wrong* (New York: St. Martin's Griffin, 1995), pp. 45–46.
10. Fred Kaplan, "Why Israel, Saudi Arabia, and Neocons Hate the Iran Deal," *Slate*, July 14, 2015.
11. John Mearsheimer and Stephen Walt, "The Israel Lobby."
12. Yitzhak Benhorin, "Israel Warned Us Against Iraq Invasion, U.S. Official Says," *Yedioth Ahronot*, September 1, 2007.
13. Yossi Alpher, "Sharon Warned Bush," *Forward*, January 12, 2007.
14. *BBC News* Staff, "Palestinians Get Saddam Funds," *BBC News*, March 13, 2003.
15. Brent Scowcroft, "Don't Attack Iraq," *Wall Street Journal*, August 15, 2002. Scowcroft writes: "Israel would have to expect to be the first casualty, as in 1991 when Saddam sought to bring Israel into the Gulf conflict. This time, using weapons of mass destruction, he might succeed, provoking Israel to respond, perhaps with nuclear weapons, unleashing an Armageddon in the Middle East."
16. Norman Podhoretz quotes John Podhoretz in *World War IV: The Long Struggle Against Islamofascism* (New York: Doubleday Books, 2007), p. 56.
17. Hillel Fendel, "Krauthammer on PA State, Obama, Pollard, and More," *Arutz Sheva*, August 8, 2010.
18. Martin Peretz and Daniel Pipes, "Bush, Clinton, & the Jews—A Debate," *Commentary*, October 1992.
19. Jeffrey Goldberg, "The Neocons Split With Israel Over Egypt," *The Atlantic*, February 2, 2011.
20. Barak Ravid, "Netanyahu Warns Outcome of Egypt Revolution Could Be Like Iran's," *Ha'aretz*, January 31, 2011.
21. Shmuel Rosner, "Why Israel Hates the Egyptian Uprising," *Slate*, February 3, 2011.
22. Editors, "About" section of *The National Interest* (http://nationalinterest.org/about-the-national-interest).
23. Interview with Norman Podhoretz.
24. Irving Kristol, "Kissinger at a Dead End," *Wall Street Journal*, March 10, 1976.
25. Richard Nixon, *1999: Victory Without War* (New York: Pocket Books, 1989), p. 276.
26. Joshua Muravchik, *The Imperative of American Leadership* (Washington, DC: American Enterprise Institute, 1996), p. 64.
27. *UN Watch*, "UN Adopts 6 Resolutions on Israel, 0 on Rest of World," November 24, 2015 (http://www.unwatch.org/un-adopts-6-resolutions-on-israel-0-on-rest-of-world/).
28. Irving Kristol, *Reflections of a Neoconservative* (New York: Basic Books, 1983), p. 230.
29. Midge Decter, "The U.N. and U.S. National Interests," *Always Right: Selected Writings of Midge Decter* (Washington, DC: The Heritage Foundation, 2002), p. 35.
30. Michael Oren, *Six Days of War: June 1967 and the Making of the Modern Middle East* (New York: Medisco Press, 2003) p. 139.
31. Norman Podhoretz, *Why Are Jews Liberal?* (New York: Doubleday Books, 2009), pp. 194–195. Podhoretz writes that Jeanne Kirkpatrick told President Reagan that she would only comply with that vote if it did not include the imposition of sanctions on Israel.
32. Robert Kagan, "American Power—A Guide for the Perplexed," *Commentary*, April 1996, p. 22.
33. Ruth Wisse, "Rising to the Occasion," *The Weekly Standard*, March 16, 2015.
34. Jonathan Tobin, "Listen to the Deafening Silence," *Commentary*, October 1, 2015.
35. Kenneth N. Waltz, "Why Iran Should Get the Bomb," *Foreign Affairs*, July/August 2012.

36. Amir Taheri, "Is Israel the Problem?," *Commentary*, February 2007, p. 36.
37. Rick Richman, "Netanyahu Must Give That Speech," *Commentary*, February 12, 2015.
38. William Kristol and Robert Kagan, "Saddam Must Go," *The Weekly Standard*, November 17, 1997, p. 220.
39. Lazar Berman, "Iran Militia Chief: Destroying Israel is Nonnegotiable," *Times of Israel*, March 31, 2015.

Chapter Three

More Concern About Liberal Democracy?

This point of view asserts that what the neoconservatives are primarily after is a global democratic peace. As Israel is the only stable "liberal democracy" in the Middle East region, neoconservatives are naturally disposed to side with it as the only nation in the region that shares America's western values. There is a post–Cold War proposition that democracies do not go to war with other democracies. First introduced by political scientists in the 1980s, it is a Wilsonian theory of international relations that has indeed inspired politicians, political advisors, and other foreign policy decision makers. The theory holds that a nation with popular sovereignty would seek peaceful, rather than aggressive, solutions to their disagreements and, at the same time, would engage in mutually beneficial economic trade with one another that would likewise prevent violent conflict. Not only would democratization create peace, then. It would also spread the benefits of modernity to less advanced nations through global free trade. While democratic peace theorists do not necessarily support forced democratization, the neoconservatives do. This was, in fact, one of the pillars of the Bush Doctrine. As Joshua Muravchik puts it in *Exporting Democracy: Fulfilling America's Destiny*, "Advancing the democratic cause can be America's most effective foreign policy in terms not merely of good deeds but of self-interest as well."[1]

The self-described "paleoconservatives" are the staunchest critics of neoconservatism from the standpoint of the Right. Included among them are Pat Buchanan, Paul Gottfried, Russell Kirk, Samuel Francis, Robert Novak, Joseph Sobran, M. E. Bradford, Claes Ryn, Stephen Tonsor, Taki Theodoracopulos, and Lew Rockwell. Other than Buchanan, who was a three-time presidential candidate and an often seen pundit, and Kirk, a major conservative intellectual, paleoconservatives are relegated to obscurity in the halls of academia and in their own periodicals and online sites, including *Chronicles* and *The American Conservative*, as well as their organizations, the John Randolph Society, the Rockford Institute, and the H. L. Mencken Club. Paleoconservatives have a reputation of being anti-Israel and are sometimes considered "anti-Semitic." The Anti-Defamation League, in fact, has an entire dossier on its website devoted to compiling what it considers to be Buchanan's anti-Semitic statements and activities. However, the anti-Semitic and anti-Israel reputations unfairly tarnish the paleoconservative movement. But a few of them, such as Buchanan and Sobran, are responsible for creating that reputation. The rest of them are merely tainted with that by association.

Buchanan, for instance, offended a lot of Jews when he spoke out in defense of John Demjanjuk, a Ukrainian accused of being "Ivan the Terrible," a long sought-after Nazi concentration camp guard who has been facing trials in Germany and Israel over the last two decades. Congressman James Traficant was also heavily involved in Demjanjuk's defense. Joshua Muravchik was enraged by Israel's decision to acquit him of the charges.[2] Although it is of course possible that it is indeed a case of mistaken identity, the question must be asked: Why does Buchanan expend so much of his time and energy on such an issue? Buchanan's answer, of course, would be that Demjanjuk's case ties into a larger problem of an over-obsession with human rights and his complaint that the neoconservatives are part of this global project. It would be easier to accept that premise if Buchanan himself did not spend so much of his own time chronicling human rights violations committed by the Israelis against Palestinians.[3] Buchanan's critics on his Demjanjuk defense, such as Gabriel Schoenfeld,[4] should note, however, that Buchanan gave Israel "eternal credit" for making the right decision to acquit him.[5]

While Buchanan and Sobran have argued that neoconservatives support Israel because of their Jewish tribal attachment to their homeland, Gottfried rejects his colleagues' equation. For Gottfried, neoconservatives support Israel not because Israel is the Jewish homeland, but because Israel is a beacon of liberal democracy in the Middle East. For Gottfried, neoconservatives are actually more interested in spreading western values than supporting the Jewish state. Since the Jewish state appears to be a country with a liberal form of government, he says the pro-Israel cause is a major component of the neoconservatives' globalist mission of spreading western values to the rest of the world. Norman Podhoretz has called Gottfried's view "the reverse of the usual assumed reason for our support for Israel."[6]

In *Leo Strauss and the Conservative Movement in America*, Gottfried writes: "In discussions of Israel or Jewish nationalism, Straussians [or neoconservatives] often sound like members of the Israeli Right or Far Right, and this has been taken as evidence that they lean right on everything else. However, the Straussian defense of Israel is pursued within the context of defending Anglo-American liberal democracy. Israel is presented as an outpost of democratic enlightenment, and its defenses by Straussians are no different than those that emanate from such Jewish liberal Democrats as Alan Dershowitz, Abe Foxman, and Rahm Emanuel."[7] While Gottfried is specifically referring to Straussians here, the broader thesis of the book equates Leo Strauss's disciples with neoconservatism.

A few important biographical points have to be made about Gottfried before this explanation is developed. Unlike other paleoconservatives, he is Jewish and has a son-in-law who served in the Israeli Defense Force. He also has many personal grievances against neoconservatives, especially Irving Kristol and Norman Podhoretz, who he claims have made efforts to harm his and other paleoconservatives' careers.[8] One example is his claim that these men used their influence at the Catholic University of America to stop his appointment in the classics department back in the 1980s on the grounds that he is "unreliable on Israel."[9] He also claims that a prominent *National Review* writer privately referred to him as "Pat Buchanan's court Jew,"[10] which, if true, is as indefensible as attacks on the neoconservatives' disloyalty to America.

Although it is true that Gottfried and Buchanan are friends and that Gottfried supported the latter's three presidential bids, the neoconservatives are wrong about Gottfried's lack of commitment to Israel. Gottfried is mostly a supporter of Israel's Likud Party.[11] He believes that Israel is "fighting for its survival" and that its "geopolitical options have been exaggerated by its critics." In a column responding to a pro-Israel libertarian journalist, Ilana Mercer, Gottfried writes: "Hamas is committed to the eradication of the 'Zionist entity' and to expelling or killing its present Jewish population. . . . The Israelis are trying to save their necks against implacable enemies, who from all indications have no desire to negotiate or strike bargains with them." He adds: "This seems to be the case, despite the fact that the neoconservatives say exactly the same thing."[12]

Gottfried also states, however, that his concern about Israel's existential crisis derives primarily from his own Jewishness and that if he were not a Jew he would instead be focused on other issues. Although, it seems that he is already focused on other issues. He writes very little in support of Israel, despite being a consummate scholar with ten books and hundreds of columns and articles to his name. In fact, wherever he does discuss Israel, it is seemingly always within the context of criticizing the neoconservative's stronghold on the American conservative movement. For Gottfried, the neoconservatives are like the broken clock that is right twice a day.

As for his views on his friend Buchanan's anti-Israel posture, while he sees his attitudes against Israel as "terrible," he still defends Buchanan.[13] He does so on the grounds that the neoconservatives would never return the favor of supporting Israel by admonishing the Left's attacks on the Catholic Church. Instead, he argues that the neoconservatives drove Buchanan away from them, rather than vice versa. The neoconservatives, he says, join the Left in vilifying the Vatican and its past popes. Buchanan was at one time actually a close ally of the neoconservatives, having once agreed with them about Israel, and even extends gratitude to Irving Kristol in the acknowledgements of his first book, *Conservative Votes, Liberal Victories*. It was not until support only seemed to be going in one direction that Buchanan, who is Catholic, turned on them.

But an important point in all this is that unlike those who allege that neoconservatives improperly have dual loyalties, Gottfried understands tribal attachment a legitimate cause of support, whether for Israel in the case of Jews or the Vatican in the case of Catholics. But he believes the neoconservatives have an illegitimate motivator. It is not for tribal reasons they support Israel, but because the Jewish state is a champion of human rights and western democratic liberalism. For them, he says, Israel meets those criteria whereas the Vatican does not.

Where neoconservatives deem him "unreliable on Israel," it is often a result of a misunderstanding of his beliefs. Gottfried does indeed like to highlight in his writings and speeches Israel's laws that consider Palestinians second-class citizens and that much of the modern state of Israel was built on land taken from Arabs. He certainly often mentions religious and cultural laws in Israel today that make it first and foremost a Jewish state founded on Jewish culture. And he argues that the real Israel actually looks nothing like what neoconservatives describe as a great bastion of civil liberty. For Gottfried, America's image of Israel is filtered through the lenses of neoconservative publications, most especially *The Jerusalem Post*.

Although not a paleoconservative herself exactly, the shock-polemicist Ann Coulter reverses the argument in her book, *Adios, America*. Coulter questions why Israel can be predicated on a single ethnic national identity while America cannot. Directed mostly at Democrats but also in part toward neoconservatives and mainstream pro-immigration Republicans, she asks the question, "Is Israel special? For some of us, America is special, too."[14]

Israel is actually a very complex society with secular and religious contradictions. But Gottfried's purpose in all this is not to criticize Israel, but rather to oppose the neoconservative view that Israel is committed to equal justice for all. Coming from Gottfried, this is not a criticism because he does not believe a good government should be committed to freedom, equality, and human rights. He believes that if a state wants to favor one heritage over all others, it has that prerogative. In that sense, Gottfried may even be more pro-Israel than the neoconservatives. The very basis of paleoconservatism is its emphasis on context and restoring the primacy of a local nation's historically-rooted traditions over the political values of the modern Enlightenment.

However, even Gottfried helps to confuse matters when he writes in Sniegoski's prologue that Bush's policy advisors were "driven by their strident Zionism." And he has only words of sympathy for Walt, Mearsheimer, and Norman Finklestein, who have taken on the "American Zionist Lobby." However, Gottfried's use of the term is very loose, and given that Sniegoski's book is for popular consumption rather than academic, and especially considering that Gottfried's role in it is to introduce the text as a prologue, he does not get very technical with semantics. He does, however, assert that the Zionism of the neoconservatives bears no relation to actual Zionist agendas in Israel and that neoconservatives are even usually frustrated by the decisions of Likud's leaders. Gottfried writes, "While neoconservatives have generally opposed the Israeli Labor Party as too soft on Israel's Arab enemies, it has also scolded Likud premiers Ariel Sharon and Ehud Olmert when they have not met neoconservative standards of being tough enough with the Palestinians or with Hezbollah in Lebanon." Most importantly, Gottfried continues: "Probably the ideal Israeli leader, from the neoconservative perspective, is Benjamin Netanyahu, for which one major reason is that this Likudnik hawk has spent considerable time in the United States and around the neoconservatives, and he slavishly imitates their rhetoric about Israel as a Middle Eastern advocate of 'global democracy.'"[15]

Aiding this view of the neoconservatives' motivations is Norman Podhoretz's agreement with George W. Bush that a pre-condition of Palestinian statehood must be that it is a democratic state.[16] However, Podhoretz himself never does support Palestinian statehood, whether democratic or authoritarian. Nor does Podhoretz believe, as Bush did, that the Palestinians are merely "pawns in the Middle East conflict"[17] who are just being used as such by a corrupt Palestinian leadership. Podhoretz writes: "Nor, alas, is it only the leaders of the Palestinians who harbor this evil intent [of wiping Israel off the map]. As revealed by poll after poll, as well as by the elections that led the way for Hamas to take power in Gaza, a decisive majority of the Palestinian people does so as well."[18]

But Podhoretz does indeed go on to say, "No doubt this is the fruit of relentless indoctrination from above, but the damage has been done, and the end result is what it is."[19] However, he rejects the notion that the majority of Palestinians want peace. Whether this is because they are brainwashed by their leaders or if they came to their hatred of Israel without their leaders' influence, a democratic Palestine would not be devoted to peace with Israel. Podhoretz, then, never endorses Palestinian statehood. While it is true that Podhoretz generally supports the democratic peace idea and calls it the "completion" of the Bush Doctrine,[20] he does not see democracy as the necessary solution to the Israeli-Palestinian conflict. As Bret Stephens would also later similarly ask, "Why doesn't the U.S. insist that Palestinian leaders prove they are capable of decently governing a state before being granted one?"[21] Pat

Buchanan, one of the harshest conservative critics of neoconservatism and of Israel, in fact agrees with Podhoretz and Stephens on this point. Buchanan writes, "Not one of the twenty-two Arab countries today qualifies as fully democratic. Yet, the more democratic they become, the more responsive their regimes must be to the will of the 'Arab Street.' Those who tell us that democracies never go to war with one another may see that proposition tested, as Arab monarchies fall to more 'democratic' regimes, as happened in Teheran with the overthrow of the shah."[22]

It would be a mistake to say that the neoconservatives—at least not all of them—are more wedded to their template of democratization than to Israel. Nor is the reverse adequate. But there are often contradictions like these that muddy the waters. In the case of the Arab Spring, the neoconservatives felt they knew better than Israel. In their eyes, Israel was wrong, despite having intelligence knowledge about Egypt's factional strife that far surpass anything the neoconservatives can possibly know about it. And yet, neoconservatives seem to be fairly confident that their plan of democratization would not work with Palestinians. They never quite explain why Palestinians are the sole exception. In his article, "Is the Bush Doctrine Dead?" Podhoretz pins that problem on President Bush but does not offer his own answer.

It is also curious that the neoconservatives understand what the majority of illiberal and nondemocratic societies in the UN General Assembly have done to exploit western principles of democracy and equality, yet still believe democracy within those societies would garner different results. In the Heritage Foundation panel, Midge Decter said:

> The United Nations as an institution was an effort to sell American values, American political values, to the world. It was an invention of the United States, and one might say in admiration of this country. . . . For it was an effort to offer to the world a model of the liberal parliamentary order. . . . Therefore it included a body, the General Assembly, which gave equal voice and equal representation to all the sovereign nations. This resulted in its being unable to reflect the realities of power in the world, which is undoubtedly one of the reasons why it has been unable to function really as a peacekeeping organization.[23]

If democracy and equal representation has failed at the UN to establish a functioning order, why would it necessarily do so within any particular country's internal government?

As for Israeli democracy, some prominent neoconservatives have expressed sympathy for the Palestinians in the hopes of seeing peace achieved and strengthening Israel's liberal democracy. This was especially the case in the Bush White House. Many of them were trying to nudge Prime Minister Olmert into a two-state solution. Paul Wolfowitz in 2002, for instance, told a large gathering of Jews at the National Mall in Washington, DC, "Innocent

Palestinians are suffering and dying in great numbers as well."[24] Wolfowitz's remark was met with jeering from the audience.

Even neoconservatives on the most pro-Israel side of the spectrum have been critical of some of Israel's policies, especially on some of the settlement construction. On the fiftieth anniversary of the Six Day War, Bret Stephens wrote a thorough reaction to the charge that Israel has been an occupier for the last fifty years, but added, "Israel is not a nation of saints and has made its mistakes. The most serious of those is proliferation of West Bank settlements beyond those in historically recognized blocs."[25] Joshua Muravchik is also critical of the settlements for much of the same reasons.[26] He is critical of Menachem Begin for starting the settlement movement. In an interview with the *Times of Israel*, Muravchick said that Begin's premise that "God gave us the land, end of discussion" was "unyielding."[27] In the same interview, he also describes Begin's war with Lebanon as a "debacle."

A prominent fellow traveler of the neoconservatives, former Secretary of State Condoleezza Rice proclaimed at the 2007 peace conference in Annapolis that "frankly, it is time for the establishment of a Palestinian state,"[28] and has purportedly compared Israeli Defense Force checkpoints with American racial segregation. As *Ha'aretz* reported in 2007: "In private conversations—and as she said in Annapolis—Rice tends to compare the Israeli occupation in the territories to the racial segregation that used to be the norm in the American South. The Israel Defense Forces checkpoints where Palestinians are detained remind her of the buses she rode as a child in Alabama, which had separate seats for blacks and whites."[29] However, these were not the views she apparently privately expressed in Bush's first term during her role as national security advisor. By the time she headed the State Department, her views shifted toward a two-state solution.[30] However, in her 2011 memoir, *No Higher Honor*, Rice later blames the breakdown of the Annapolis talks on Palestinian leader Mahmoud Abbas for failing to accept Olmert's concessions.[31]

Gottfried's paleoconservative argument is more rare to find than the position that neoconservatives support Israel just out of loyalty to a Jewish state. But another proponent of this point of view is the left-wing anti-Zionist blogger, Philip Weiss. In describing the neoconservative stance on Hamas and Fatah, he writes that neoconservatives think that: "If Arab countries were converted by force into democracies, the people would embrace the change and would also accept Israel as a great neighbor." Weiss continues: "It's a variation on a neocolonialist theory that pro-Israel ideologues have believed going back to the 1940s: that Palestinians would accept a Jewish state if you got rid of their corrupt leadership and allowed the people to share in Israel's modern economic miracle. The evidence for this causation is at every hand."[32]

Neoconservatives themselves emphasize their motivation to promote democracy, citing the fact that during the Cold War and especially during the 1980s, their focus was on regions outside of the Middle East. Max Boot writes, "The charge that neocons are concerned above all with the welfare of Israel is patently false. In the 1980s, they were the leading proponents of democratization in places as disparate as Nicaragua, Poland, and South Korea." Boot also goes on to challenge the charge that neoconservatives are simply out to fight wars against Muslims. He adds, "In the 1990s, they were the most ardent champions of intervention in Bosnia and Kosovo—missions designed to rescue Muslims, not Jews."[33]

Gottfried's explanation for Buchanan's drift away from the neoconservatives differs from Timothy Stanley's, who in his biography of Buchanan, *The Crusader*, says that Buchanan's prior support for Israel and his alliance with the neoconservatives were Cold War phenomena. Stanley writes, "When Israel lost its strategic significance to the U.S. after 1989, Pat became an open critic."[34] After 1989, Buchanan began to evaluate America's interests as more closely aligning with the Palestinians than with the Israelis. In *The Washington Times*, Buchanan asks, "What vital interest of ours is advanced by subsidizing a policy that denies to Palestinians that God-given right to a homeland, a flag and a state of their own, that Americans have championed all over the world, all of our lives?" Buchanan also adds, "Israeli troops killed hundreds of men, women, and children; they have beaten, wounded, maimed some 25,000; they have dynamited homes, and imprisoned, without trial, thousands of Palestinians. Were that the price of holding onto Puerto Rico, most of us, long ago, would have said: Let them go."[35]

But what is peculiar about Buchanan's stance on the Israeli-Palestinian conflict is that he abandons his usual journalistic standards. He neglects to mention that Palestinians put civilians on the frontlines of combat as human shields, making it impossible for the Israeli soldiers to avoid committing violence against them. And yes, it is probably true that if that were the price of holding onto Puerto Rico, most Americans would have probably decided it was not worth it. But that is a greatly imbalanced comparison, as what Israel has sought to defend is far more significant to the Israelis than Puerto Rico is to the United States. If this were the price of holding onto California or Texas, Americans—and likely Buchanan—would be more supportive of forceful action. Additionally, Buchanan's position on this conflict is atypical of his views on other conflicts over control of land. In what other instance does he emphasize the principle of the "God-given right" to a homeland over other interests? When Vladimir Putin annexed the Crimea from Ukraine, he said, "Putin's actions, though unsettling, are not irrational."[36] So why does Buchanan not view Israel's actions in the same light, as unsettling but not irrational? In the same article, he rationalizes Putin's actions on the fact that 60 percent of Crimeans, if asked to go to the polls to express their will on the matter, would vote to return under Russian control rather than stay part of Ukraine. But on what basis does he consider a people's will to self-determination can be determined? In other issues, he decries the neoconservative and liberal emphasis on democracy as the definitive standard, but here he supports majority rule as the deciding factor, and without even a popular consensus—just merely a majority will of 60 percent.

And where else does Buchanan have such humanitarian concerns about a "third world" people who are causing such problems, much less existential ones, for a western country? The most obvious case in point is Buchanan's positions on illegal immigration from Mexico into the United States. In his book, *State of Emergency*, he says that both parties' failure—or, what he calls, "moral rot,"—to resolve the crisis of the "third world invasion" is attributed to their being so "terrified of being called 'nativist,' 'xenophobic,' or even 'racist' that they blind themselves to the rampant criminality along our southern frontier."[37] He also continues through the book to chastise both Democrats and Republicans for maintaining "sanctuary cities" and being willing accomplices to illegal immigration. In *The Death of the West*, his treatise warning of third world demographic shifts in many countries that threaten the survival of the West, Buchanan includes Israel's Palestinian problem as among the primary examples, devoting an entire section of the book to that problem. This of course does not necessarily imply that he should agree with the hardline policies of the Likud government; the position could in fact be a defense of stopping settlement construction and giving land concessions so that Israel no longer has so many Palestinians under its jurisdiction. However, these are also the views of many prominent neoconservatives, albeit not all, who supported the Kadima party's 2003 disengagement from the Gaza for very similar reasons. Moreover, Buchanan's case against Israel is largely predicated on his evaluation of the Jewish state as serving little in common with American interests. But clearly he does see Israel as part of the West and conceptualizes "western interests" as something that are common to both countries.

One of the fairest oppositional volumes against the neoconservatives is *The Legacy of George W. Bush's Foreign Policy: Moving Beyond Neoconservatism*, by Ilan Peleg, a scholar at LaFayette College. What makes Peleg's book a good one is that he does not resort to derision or accuse them of ulterior motives, conspiracy, or greed. Israel is hardly mentioned in it, and never named as a justification for their goals. Rather, he carefully and critically analyzes the neoconservative foreign policy model and its theoretical underpinnings. Peleg notes the unusual mixture of optimism and pessimism in neoconservative thinking.[38] On one hand they see the world through a very dark lens, as a war of all against all, and doubt the capacity of human beings to reason their way through problems. On the other, they confidently assert that everyone ultimately wants freedom and democracy and is capable of cooperation. In that regard, it is a hybrid of realism and liberal internationalism, an odd but nevertheless very real combination of cynical Hobbesianism and hopeful Kantianism. It has its roots in realism, but like Irving Kristol does with capitalism, they withhold one cheer.

Peleg also believes the neoconservatives are radicals. He writes: "This radicalism has been reflected in complete and total rejection of the status quo in world politics (and to some extent in domestic American politics), as well as in the ambitious, far-reaching plans of the neoconservatives."[39] Their paleoconservative opponents like Gottfried and Buchanan would certainly disagree with Peleg on the domestic side. Neoconservatives have accepted the status quo on America's immigration policies. They have either given up or have chosen not to fight as hard anymore for the social and conservative cultural issues such as traditional marriage, school vouchers, and ending affirmative action. In 1992, Irving Kristol proclaimed the culture war lost.[40] Neoconservatives also mildly accept the welfare state, seeking to reform it rather than abolish it.[41] But on the foreign policy side, Peleg does have a point that the neoconservatives usually prefer major changes to accepting the status quo. They are problem-solvers, but their solutions to problems often—although only in the certain regions of the world—involve grand-scale, transformative changes by the use of military force. And on the matter of the Israeli-Palestinian conflict, they certainly do seem poised to accept a stalemate. Even on the Iranian agreement they would be more favorable to accepting the status quo of keeping sanctions in place than have the United States agree to the deal John Kerry negotiated.

NOTES

1. Joshua Muravchik, *Exporting Democracy* (Washington, DC: American Enterprise Institute Press, 1992), p. 6.
2. Joshua Muravchik, "John Demjanjuk: A Summing Up," *Commentary*, April 1, 1997.
3. See for example Pat Buchanan, "Zionism's Dead End," antiwar.com, June 28, 2008. He apparently gave this as a talk at the Conference for the Right of Return and the Secular Democratic State in Haifa on June 21 of that year.
4. Gabriel Schoenfeld, *The Return of Anti-Semitism* (New York: Encounter Books, 2005), p. 113.
5. Pat Buchanan, "The Persecution of John Demjanjuk," *Townhall*, May 13, 2011.
6. Interview with Norman Podhoretz.
7. Paul Gottfried, *Leo Strauss and the Conservative Movement in America* (United Kingdom: Cambridge University Press, 2011), p. 69–70.
8. The most well known example is Irving Kristol's role in 1982 in convincing Ronald Reagan to withdraw M. E. Bradford's nomination as the director of the National Endowment for the Humanities.
9. Interview with Norman Podhoretz.
10. Interview with Paul Gottfried.
11. Ibid.
12. Paul Gottfried, *War and Democracy* (Hungary: Arktos Media Limited, 2012), p. 120.
13. Interview with Paul Gottfried.

14. Ann Coulter, *Adios, America: The Left's Plan to Turn Our Country into a Third World Hell-Hole* (New York: Regnery Press, 2015).

15. Paul Gottfried, prologue to Stephen J. Sniegoski, *The Transparent Cabal: The Neoconservative Agenda, War in the Middle East, and the National Interest of Israel* (United States: Enigma Editions, 2008), pp. xii–xiii.

16. Norman Podhoretz, "Is the Bush Doctrine Dead?," *Commentary*, September 2006, p. 19.

17. Ibid.

18. Norman Podhoretz, "Pity the Palestinians? Count Me Out," *Wall Street Journal*, April 9. 2014.

19. Ibid.

20. "Is the Bush Doctrine Dead?," p. 19.

21. Bret Stephens, "Israel Looks Beyond America," *Wall Street Journal*, February 15, 2016.

22. Patrick J. Buchanan, *The Death of the West: How Dying Populations and Immigrant Invasions Imperil Our Country and Civilization* (New York: St. Martin's Griffin, 2002), p. 116.

23. Midge Decter, "The U.N. and U.S. National Interests," *Always Right: Selected Writings of Midge Decter,* ed. Philip N. Truluck (Washington, DC: The Heritage Foundation, 2002), p. 35.

24. Frank Rich, "The Booing of Wolfowitz," *New York Times*, May 11, 2002.

25. Bret Stephens, "The Nonsense of '50 Years of Occupation' By Israel," *Pittsburgh Post-Gazette*, June 6, 2017.

26. Interview with Joshua Muravchik.

27. Gary Rosenblatt, "How the World Turned Against Israel," *Times of Israel*, May 13, 2015.

28. Associated Press, "Rice: 'It's Time' for a Palestinian State," *NBC News*, October 15, 2007.

29. Aluf Benn, "What's the Hurry," *Ha'Aretz*, December 27, 2007.

30. Elisabeth Bumiller, "Rice's Turnabout in Mideast Talks," *New York Times*, November, 26, 2007.

31. However, Mahmoud Abbas tells a different story, blaming Israel instead for the failure of the talks. See Zvika Krieger, "What Condi Rice's Memoir Gets Wrong (and Right) on Israel," *The Atlantic*, October 27, 2011.

32. Philip Weiss, "The U.S. is At Last Facing the Neocon Captivity," *Mondoweiss*, May 19, 2015 (http://mondoweiss.net/2015/05/facing-neocon-captivity/).

33. Max Boot, "Myths About Neoconservatism," *The Neocon Reader*, ed. Irwin Stelzer (New York: Grove Press, 2004), p. 48.

34. Timothy Stanley, *The Crusader: The Life and Tumultuous Times of Pat Buchanan* (New York: Thomas Dunne Books, 2012), p. 137.

35. Ibid.

36. Patrick J. Buchanan, "Resist the War Party on Crimea," *The American Conservative*, March 4, 2014.

37. Patrick J. Buchanan, *State of Emergency* (New York: St. Martin's Griffin, 2007), p. 8.

38. Ilan Peleg, *The Legacy of George W. Bush's Foreign Policy: Moving Beyond Neoconservatism* (New York: Routledge, 2009), p. 60.

39. Ibid, p. 53.

40. Stephen Prothero, "They'll always lose the culture wars: The right loves fighting lost causes– but liberals keep winning," *Salon*, January 31, 2016. Also see William F. Buckley, *In Search of Anti-Semitism*, p. 126. Kristol wrote to William F. Buckley: "Pat Buchanan is seeking to shape the conservative movement along reactionary lines. And behind him there has formed a curious coalition of what have been called 'paleo-conservatives'—i.e., conservatives of the 1930s–1950s vintage. . . . These people really do want to turn the clock a long way's back—a proper aesthetic agenda but never a serious political agenda."

41. Irving Kristol, "A Conservative Welfare State," *Wall Street Journal*, June 14, 1993.

Chapter Four

Because They Are American Jews

Commentary's mission statement does not mention Israel at all. It refers to America and to the Jewish people but says nothing directly about Israel. It reads: "Since 1945, *Commentary* has been, as our founder, Elliot Cohen wrote at that time, 'an act of affirmation.' It remains an expression of belief in the United States, perhaps most of all in America's central role in the preservation and advance of Western civilization and, most immediately, the continuing existence of the Jewish people. *Commentary*, in the words of Cohen, 'is an act of faith in our possibilities in America.'" That mission statement encapsulates the neoconservative mind quite aptly.

In an interview, Gottfried said that there is, in fact, a similarity between the neoconservatives' support for Israel and many Americans' pro-Britain Anglo attitudes during World War I.[1] In both cases, they are driven by both a deep ancestral attachment to another country and by the rhetoric of "global democracy." In that sense, Gottfried sees a dual purpose of a Wilsonian foreign policy agenda. In fact, as misplaced as his animus against neoconservatives may be about these matters, Gottfried has the best and most accurate understanding within his paleoconservative coterie of what drives them toward supporting a pro-Israel foreign policy.

Gottfried is largely correct that the neoconservatives see Israel as reflecting American values, but he is wrong to discount their tribal attachment. But it is a different kind of tribal attachment. It derives more from their *American* Jewish experience than anything else. What so many opponents of the neoconservatives miss is that these are men and women who fully embrace their American identity just as much as they do their Jewishness. And this is true for the vast majority of American Jews—Sephardic and Ashkenazi, Orthodox, Conservative, Reform, and unaffiliated. Irving Kristol wrote an essay titled, "The Future of American Jewry," in which he reflected on the convergence of Jewishness and American identity as being an extraordinary amongst the world's Jewry. During the years after 1948, the United States had among the lowest number of émigrés to Israel, comparable to that of other countries, and there were still a lot of Russian and East European Jews who wanted to come to America rather than Israel. The Jews of other nations who remain in them feel more uncomfortable with their gentile surroundings. In Europe, secular Jews make a great effort to distance themselves from their Jewish ancestry in order to assimilate, while religious ones live a far more insular and detached existence, eschewing assimilation altogether. Kristol writes: "Analysts of American Jewry look at their subject with a European paradigm in mind. But the United States is an exceptional country, and Jewish history elsewhere throws very little light on the American Jewish experience in the 20th Century."[2]

They support the Likud Party because of its relative closeness to American-style conservatism. If the neoconservatives were the "militant Zionists" their critics deem them to be, there are plenty of other more suitable Israeli political parties they would support, including Naftali Bennett's The Jewish Home and Avigdor Lieberman's Yisrael Beteinu. But the neoconservatives are often critical of Bennett and Lieberman, while almost always supporting the more centrist Benjamin Netanyahu. While its critics portray Likud as a vastly right-wing Zionist party, its platform is actually the most moderate within the right-wing bloc. On non-security related issues it has a laissez-faire approach to the domestic economy and a tepid embrace of religious values. In that way, Likud is not so dissimilar to the Republican Party in the United States.

Norman Podhoretz has also argued that the argument about Israel's catalytic role in defining America's Middle Eastern foreign policy is—at least from the Left and in Europe—often disingenuous. He believes a lot of the animosity toward Israel is actually a veiled abhorrence of the United States. In *World War IV*, he writes:

> Indeed, the hatred of Israel was in large part a surrogate for anti-Americanism, rather than the reverse. Israel was seen as the spearhead of the American drive for domination over the Middle East. As such, the Jewish state was a translation of America into, as it were, Hebrew—the "little enemy," the "little Satan." To rid the region of it would thus be tantamount to cleansing an area belonging to Islam (*dar al-Islam*) or the blasphemous political, social, and cultural influences emanating from a barbaric and murderous force. But the force, so to speak, was with America, of which Israel was merely an instrument.[3]

Whether or not he is right that the animus against Israel is rooted more in anti-Americanism than vice versa, the key point is that Podhoretz interprets it that way. For him, Israel is an extension of the American exceptionalism.

Adversaries of both countries despise this, he believes, for what they regard as a mutual smug arrogance.

Like America, neoconservatives see Israel as a place people go to escape persecution. Jews flock there from all over the world, coming from places where they are not permitted to freely practice their religion, or worse, murdered. But it is not just Jews who go to Israel for this reason. Israel absorbs Christians and even Arabs who are looking for a similar safe haven. In a way, their fondness for Israel is the reverse of how they imagine America's beginnings. While America was the "New Israel," modern Israel is the "New America." Both countries are promised lands in a world filled with so much evil and treachery.

Jonathan Tobin notes the high number of homosexual Arabs who immigrate to Israel. Despite the fact that Jewish *Halacha* condemns homosexuality just as much as Islamic *Sharia* does, Israel is still an open society where citizens are free to violate Jewish divine law far more often than not. And whether there are legally enforced religious conventions or not on a given matter, either way there is intense strife between Israel's religious and secular communities as a result of it. Inasmuch as Israel entangles synagogue and state on a whole host of matters, including having Shabbat closing laws, subsidies for the rabbinate, and having no civil marriage, Israel is not anywhere near the kind of theocratic regime its critics pretend it to be. Tobin writes:

> Israel is a free country, something you wouldn't know if your only view of the Jewish state was delivered to you by mainstream media coverage. The anti-Israel crowd can call mentions of gay rights "pink washing." But all that means is that they don't wish to acknowledge the difference between Israeli and Palestinian cultures.[4]

Where neoconservatives are critical of Israel, it is often in cases in which the Jewish state fails to live up to American standards of a free society. For example, Tobin was critical of the Knesset's proposed defunding of organizations that denigrate the Israel Defense Forces (IDF) or support the Boycott, Divestment, Sanctions (BDS) movement. Tobin considers it "deeply problematic" that, "unlike the United States, Israel has no First Amendment protections of speech, so it is legally possible for the Knesset to cut left-wing NGOs off from foreign funding or even to ban them outright. That's something that couldn't happen in the United States."[5] Tobin disapproves of this, even while condemning these groups for "subversion" and "undermining the [democratic] foundations of the state."

Israel may indeed be a complex and unordinary society but the neoconservatives know that it still has all of the virtues and vices of any western society. That it has its own unique iniquities does not negate that fact. But they tend to be more concerned about common problems over those that are extraordinary to Israel. This includes not just Islam-inspired terrorism, but left-wing ideologies too. Israel has its radical Leftist elements just like the United States. And, just like the United States, radicalism emanates from about the same social quarters, such as the media and the academy. Not only does it have groups that delegitimize its very existence, it has radical pacifists, feminists, a gay rights movement, multiculturalists, environmentalists, and socialists and trade unionists. Because of its socialist past, Israel suffers from even greater bureaucratization and labor conglomeration as the United States does, as well as big government hindrances on economic innovation. Just like in America or in any European country, radical ideologies flourish in Israel. Israel may not be a society founded on liberty, but its citizens have enough *de facto* liberty to organize for radical social change. And given Israel's great diversity of ethnicity, religious beliefs, languages, and tribal customs, the ideological divide is even more deeply rooted in Israel than it is in America. Israel's political spectrum is far more complicated than American-style juxtaposition between liberal and conservative.

Neoconservatives, however, devote much criticism to the Israeli politics in which they can relate to as conservative Americans. Just like they are critical of the radical environmental Left here at home, they are frustrated by the same phenomena in Israel. For example, after the discovery of the natural gas fields, *Commentary* ran an opinion-editorial by Arthur Herman who was exasperated by the environmentalists who protested against drilling.[6] The natural gas discovery is an economic game-changer that is certain to greatly enrich Israel and yet environmentalists do not want Israel to exploit it. On the presence of feminism, *Commentary*'s Evelyn Gordon criticized Israel's "Women of the Wall" movement.[7] This was a movement of Reform and Conservative women in 2013 who were insisting upon having the right to wear *tallit* and phylacteries and pray at the Western Wall with the orthodox men.

But what is most noteworthy about both of these cases is that both Herman and Gordon seem more concerned about how Israel's management of these problems would affect diplomatic relations with the United States than they are about the radicalism itself. The drilling would have been done as a partnership with a Texas oil company, and unaffiliated American Jews cannot relate to what all this fuss is about with the "Women of the Wall." These two problems seem to concern Tobin more than the very existence of these radical movements in Israel. Gottfried is therefore partially correct that neoconservatives see Israel as being linked to an American foreign policy agenda, but they certainly do not approve of advancing radical domestic reforms in either country. These issues are just less important to them than maintaining a strong American-Israeli relationship.

Norman Podhoretz disliked the socialist ideology among the Zionists. He writes in *My Love Affair With America* that he would get into debates with them about which country was better, America or Israel, and would be told that American Jews are "too materialistic," and "too deeply sunk in the flesh pots of a rich country, to make the sacrifices in [their] standard of living that emigrating to Israel would entail."[8] But neoconservatives take it as a badge of pride in the Jewish state that it has moved away considerably from its socialist design, and that even the *kibbutzim* have become competitive business ventures. They are proud of Israel's international reputation as the "start up nation."

When Netanyahu came to Washington, DC to speak before a joint session of Congress in 2015—at the strong disapproval of the Obama administration—neoconservatives such as Bill Kristol saw in the prime minister's message something that resonates as both distinctly American and Israeli. Kristol wrote: "One also couldn't help noticing that Netanyahu quoted only the first part of Deuteronomy 31:6. He left unsaid the remainder of the verse: 'For the Lord your God Himself marches with you.' Jews and Christians trust that this is the case—just as Americans profess, 'In God We Trust.' But in neither Israel nor America do we simply trust in divine providence. In both, 'we the people' have to act, as best we can and on behalf of what is right 'as God gives us to see the right' as God gives us to see the right.' Here too one was reminded of the deep kinship between the two nations, the United States and Israel."[9]

Netanyahu's words seem to have moved Kristol deeply, however there is likely a lot to what Bibi said that was crafted for political theater. Netanyahu was criticized in Israel for accepting Speaker of the House John Boehner's invitation to speak before Congress. Many feared that it would alienate Israel even more with the Obama administration and the Democrats in Congress and that Israel would ultimately get nothing in the Iran agreement that would ever allow them to act if Iran reaches a certain threshold on its nuclear program. But he is a masterful orator because he knows what to say to arouse the right sentiments in Americans, particularly Christian Americans. And to a great extent, *The Weekly Standard* does the same because of its more gentile audience relative to *Commentary*'s, which is more commonly read by Jews. *The Weekly Standard*, however, reaches a much larger Christian audience and therefore defends Israel before a very different segment of America. It is unknown whether this is accidental or by design, but Kristol and his staff do seem to be genuine believers that the destinies of the two countries are intrinsically linked.

Neoconservatives do feel a tribal attachment toward Israel, but that attachment is more often reflected in their defense against Israel's dishonest assailers than in their foreign policy positions. When it is a question of what America must do, they think primarily as Americans, seeing Israel as an important component of the American mission. Certainly, as Jews, they are proud that Israel is of such a pivotal importance in their quest for a liberal democratic global order. They may often be wrong about that but it is their contention nonetheless. But on matters relating to the demonization, delegitimation, and double standards placed on the Jewish state, those indeed tug at their heartstrings as Jews. Their Christian friends likewise feel compelled to help fend off undo attacks on Israel, agreeing that when Israel is vilified, Jews are vilified.

These assailments on Israel happen on a routine basis in the media, university campuses, and by American and foreign leaders. Ruth Wisse, a neoconservative professor of Jewish literature at Harvard, was livid in 1982 when *The Spokesman Review* ran a story about Israel suppressing the free press of Palestinian poetry. The story was found to be lacking any substantive basis due to misinformation that could have been verified if the author had done his job as a journalist and authenticated it. That in and of itself could have just been chalked up to incompetent journalism if it were not for the wider context of the author's story. The author used it in a broader narrative about Israel's vast acts of censorship, which would have U.S. Justice Louis Brandeis, a proud Zionist, rolling in his grave.

The author, Anthony Lewis, writes: "Brandeis was the great American Zionist of his day. It is hard not to imagine how he would feel now about the practice of political censorship by the state for whose birth he so passionately worked."[10] Like many dishonest narratives about Israel, he craftily couches his false condemnation inside insincere reverence for the Zionist cause, giving his narrative an aura of affection for the aims of Zionism. Wisse notes the double standard as well:

> Why, if Lewis is so concerned for the Palestinian poets, did he not investigate their political rights when he was in Jordan? Hath not an Arab eyes? Shall the students and writers of Arab countries, where there are no Jews to "oppress" them with the rights of free speech, and no Jewish critics to needle the government on their behalf, be doomed to a lifetime of self-censorship of silence? It is the peculiar evil of this double standard of judgment not merely to apply an absolute moral criterion to the Jews alone, and use it as a bludgeon against the Jewish state, but to discard moral standards altogether when it comes to other nations in the region.[11]

Joshua Muravchik's book, *Making David Into Goliath*, is a good representation of the neoconservative angst over the world community's demonization of Israel and the Left's encouragement of this perception. Israel was lauded and defended by the Left when it was a younger, weaker state than it is now and when Jews were seen as the underdogs. Interestingly, as Israel has become more powerful and harder to intimidate, it has been the political Right that has championed its cause and the Left that has become increasingly opposed. This may be, to a great extent, attributed to the contradicting dispositions of Right and Left. While, the Left is usually compelled to view the weak as always the victim and the strong as always the bully, the Right generally respects strength and pluck. Israel has "pulled itself up by its own bootstraps," in their eyes. Jewish neoconservatives take pride in knowing that it was *their* people who have done that.

But that still does not explain the double standards. China is also strong and the Tibetans are also weak, yet in that case it is China that is truly guilty of violating the Tibetans' human rights. As Muravchik puts it, "Were China to grant the Tibetans what Israel has offered the Palestinians the Dalai Lama would have danced for joy."[12] And the Tibetans also do not commit nearly the same level of terrorist violence against Chinese civilians as Hamas does against Israelis. The Chinese government has never displaced its citizens from their homes to make way for a Tibetan autonomous territory, as the Israelis did in Gaza. But the time devoted by the media, the academy, and international institutions to condemning Israel is vastly higher than to criticizing China. In addition, there are many more stateless nations in the world besides the Palestinians that are seeking self-determination but receive next to no reportage by the mainstream press. In *The Weekly Standard*, Muravchik also asks: "As for thwarted national fulfillment, who is angry on behalf of the Kurds? Kurds are five times more numerous than Palestinians. Their national identity goes back a millennium while Palestinian nationalism is less than a century old. The Kurds have their own language(s), history and traditions. The Kurds yearn for a state of their own. And yet no one non-Kurdish seems to give a fig."[13]

When Jimmy Carter's book, *Peace Not Apartheid* came out in 2006, there was actually less of a reaction than one would expect from neoconservatives. In fact, despite its controversial and provocative title declaring Israel an apartheid state, the book does present criticism of Palestinian leaders and the terror groups, Hamas and Hezbollah. Carter, however, holds Israel significantly more responsible for the ongoing conflict and the failure of the cease-fires. The strongest oppositional reaction, at least in print, came from Muravchik, who responded with a lengthy piece in *Commentary*, directed more at Carter himself than at his book. Muravchik's essay was titled, "Our Worst Ex-President." Noting overwhelming bias toward Arabs on the part of the former president, Muravchik writes, "For someone who once played and still fancies himself in the role of mediator, Carter's visceral attitudes to the two sides are strikingly disparate. He finds something to like in every Arab leader he meets." Muravchik adds: "No such emotional connection, certainly, characterizes Carter's feelings about most Israeli leaders he meets—including Golda Meir, Menachem Begin, Yitzhak Shamir, Ehud Barak, Ariel Sharon, and Ehud Olmert. Universally, they seem rather to evoke his dislike, and Israel as a whole seems to have the same effect on him." Muravchik also notes that Carter seems to blindly accept Yasser Arafat's false claim that, "The PLO has never advocated the annihilation of Israel. The Zionists started the 'drive the Jews into the sea' slogan and attributed it to the PLO."[14]

Muravchik also observes Carter's inconsistent condemnations and downright fabrications of the status of Judaism in Israel. On one hand, Carter complains in *Peace Not Apartheid* of the scarcity of religion in Israel, which of course is untrue. On the other hand, he bemoans, "Very conservative religious parties [are] granted almost exclusive control over all forms of worship." Reacting to this in a footnote, Muravchik calls this "nonsense." He writes, "Religious authorities maintain control over various public and legal functions, such as Sabbath operations of government services or marriage and conversion, not over 'worship,' and the authority of Christian and Muslim clergy is recognized as applying to members of those faiths."[15] In an interview, Muravchik also says that it is important to distinguish between Israel as a *nationally* Jewish country as opposed to a *religiously* Jewish one. Israel, as he sees it, does not favor one mode of worship over all others, but rather, one people over all others are held as culminating its national identity.[16] And while Israel has been criticized for its status as a Jewish state and for featuring the Star of David on its flag, he also says that there are many other liberal democratic, and multi-ethnic countries that give precedence to one particular national heritage. For example, Israel is not the only liberal democracy to grant "right of return" to one ethnic group. Romania, Moldova, Ukraine, and Germany have had, or still have, the same.[17]

Carter's 2009 article in the *Washington Post* is even more condemnatory and presented nothing of Israel's case. Carter describes the Palestinians as in a "nonviolent civil rights struggle" and compares their aims and tactics to those of Martin Luther King, Mahatma Ghandi, and Nelson Mandela. He even goes so far as to claim that Palestinians are so desperate for peace that they are willing to live in a single democratic state alongside Jews.[18] The following day, Elliot Abrams responded with a piece of his own in the same newspaper.

Ruth Wisse notes Eugene Rostow's statement on Israeli control of post-1967 disputed territories, that one of the two pillars necessary for eventually giving those up is "recognition by the Arab states of Israel's right to live in peace within secure and recognized boundaries, free from threats or acts of force." Wisse writes:

> Rostow explains why the question of Israel's presence in the disputed territories had to be linked to Arab acceptance of Israel's presence, as if something as elementary as the need for Arab recognition should have required explanation. Israel was never in the past and in the future will never be able to "settle" Palestinian Arabs successfully or accommodate them politically without first being guaranteed unconditionally its own right to flourish.[19]

Neoconservatives such as Wisse support the eventual establishment of a Palestinian state but such statehood, they feel, must hinge first on Israel being their accepted neighbor. As they see little sign of that happening in either the near or distant future, neoconservatives do not see much of a chance of Palestinian statehood.

Although, one might say that the disproportionate attention to Israel has a philo-Semitic tenor. Perhaps the anger is directed primarily at Israel because better is expected of Jews, the "People of the Book." Critics have said that the Jews ought to act better, especially considering the severe persecution and torment *they* went through. When they are compared to Nazis, perhaps it is with the intent of provoking their guilt in light of the experience of the Holocaust. The message may be: you the oppressed are now the oppressors. And the fact that Israel is indeed seen as a Western-style liberal democracy may warrant special condemnation. A country with so much modern advancement that provides so much freedom for a vast portion of its citizens should not be limiting such freedoms to one sector of its society alone. This perspective might account for perhaps some of the emphasis on Israel's blockade of Gaza but not Egypt's along its Gaza border. This is the view expressed by Peter Beinart in *The Crisis of Zionism*. Beinart accepts the need for the Jews to be empowered by a state of their own, but writes, "Surely now, Jews can temper the single-minded pursuit of power with a concern for that power's ethical character."[20] But neoconservatives consider this explanation for the American Jewish Left's disaffection for Israel to be akin to anti-Americanism. From the neoconservative point of view, liberals do this because it is easier to blame the West than to focus condemnation at the world's true human rights abusers. This is how they account for the decline of concern for Israel that is happening on the American Jewish Left.[21]

Neoconservatives were also indignant toward the Obama administration for implying that the increased level of hostility against Israel is somehow *Israel*'s fault. Secretary of State John Kerry went to Jerusalem in 2014 and told officials, "You see for Israel there's an increasing delegitimization campaign that has been building up," citing the Palestinian conflict as its main cause, adding, "There are talks of boycotts and other kinds of things. Today's status quo absolutely, to a certainty, I promise you 100 percent, cannot be maintained."[22] The Obama administration believes strongly that if that conflict is finally settled once and for all, Israel will no longer be the target of the world community's ire as it has been. Jude Wanniski of the *Wall Street Journal*, who is typically an ally to neoconservatives on economic issues but a bitter rival on the foreign policy front, stated:

> If Israel were at peace with a friendly, neighborly Palestinian state, all of the reasons Osama bin Laden gives for his war against America and the West would be dissolved. I'm not saying the Muslim extremists would embrace

Israelis, only that their hatred would first turn to mere suspicion and dislike, which are human emotions that do not lead to suicide bombings.[23]

To the neoconservatives, these assessments are wrong in that they are oblivious to the far more deep-seeded antagonism against Israel that is caused by the simple fact that it is the *Jewish* state, and that this fact itself stymies all chances of peace with the Palestinians.

Neoconservatives do in fact believe Israel to be an exemplar of liberal democracy and therefore exceptional. But more than just symbolizing Western values, it is the only liberal democracy that is so susceptible to extinction. No other small liberal democracy has so many ardent enemies both within its borders and surrounding them who not only pledge consistently to destroy it will not even recognize its sovereign existence. But it is not just for this reason that all neoconservatives are so alarmed. Some believe the extinction of Israel would befall all Jewry, as Krauthammer has argued. Assimilation and intermarriage have so doomed the diaspora that Israel is the last, best hope for the perpetuation of the Jews.

Critics of Israel's occupation of Palestinians argue that Israel will be neither Jewish nor democratic if the occupation continues. In *The Crisis of Zionism*, Peter Beinart argues that mistreatment of another population is not "Jewish," and having millions of people under Israel's control in Gaza, East Jerusalem, and the West Bank who are not citizens and thus cannot vote is undemocratic. Beinart writes, "What the American Jewish establishment doesn't grasp is that Israel's legitimacy is bound up within its democratic character. The best way to preserve Israeli democracy, and thus marginalize those who oppose even a democratic Jewish state." Beinart continues, "Entrenching the occupation, by contrast, will gradually bring what American Jewish leaders most fear: the delegitimation of Israel as a Jewish state. The less democratic Zionism becomes in practice, the more people across the world will question the legitimacy of Zionism itself."[24]

John Kerry, in his farewell speech as secretary of state, said similarly, "If the choice is one state, Israel can either be Jewish or democratic, it cannot be both, and it won't ever really be at peace."[25] The point is sound considering the demographics. Sergio Della Pergola, a demographer at Hebrew University, estimated in early 2018 that the Jewish and Arab populations have reached near parity.[26] Arab citizens within the Green Line are Israeli citizens and have voting rights, whereas those in the territories do not. The problem makes a two-state solution increasingly necessary in order to justify Israel's standing as a liberal democratic society. However, neoconservatives do, ideally, favor a two-state solution, but they do not blame Israel for the failure of the Oslo Accords or the inability of a Palestinian state to be established.

NOTES

1. Interview with Paul Gottfried.
2. Irving Kristol, "The Future of American Jewry," in *Neoconservatism: An Autobiography of an Idea* (New York: The Free Press, 1995), p. 444.
3. Norman Podhoretz, *World War IV: The Long Struggle Against Islamo-Fascism* (New York: Doubleday, 2007), pp. 91–92.
4. Jonathan S. Tobin, "Pinkwashing? Gay Rights Shows the Difference Between Israel and Palestinians," *Commentary*, April 20, 2012.
5. Jonathan S. Tobin, "Who Opposes Democracy in Israel?" *Commentary*, December 22, 2015.
6. Arthur Herman, "Will Israel Be the Next Energy Superpower?" *Commentary*, March 1, 2014. Also see Jonathan S. Tobin, "How a Court Sank Israel's Economy," *Commentary*, March 28, 2016.
7. Evelyn Gordon, "Provocation at the Wall," *Commentary*, September 1, 2013.
8. Norman Podhoretz, *My Love Affair With America*, p. 53.
9. William Kristol, "Speaking for Israel—And America," *The Weekly Standard*, March 16, 2015.
10. Anthony J. Lewis, "Israel's Censorship Would Gall Brandeis," *The Spokesman Review*, May 21, 1982.
11. Ruth Wisse, "The Deligitimation of Israel," in *The Essential Neoconservative Reader*, ed. Mark Gerson (Boston, MA: Addison-Wesley Publishing Company, 1996), p. 198.
12. Joshua Muravchik, *Making David Into Goliath* (New York: Encounter Books, 2014), p. xi.
13. Joshua Muravchik, "Here's How the World Turned Against Israel," *The Weekly Standard*, December 2, 2014.
14. Joshua Muravchik, "Our Worst Ex-President," *Commentary*, February 2007, p. 23.
15. Ibid, p. 24.
16. Interview with Joshua Muravchik.
17. Joshua Muravchik cites C. Dumbrava, *Nationality, Citizenship, and Ethno-Cultural Belonging: Preferential Membership Belongings in Europe*.
18. Jimmy Carter, "The Elders' View of the Middle East," *Washington Post*, September 6, 2009.
19. Ruth Wisse, *If I am Not for Myself: The Liberal Betrayal of the Jews* (New York: The Free Press, 1992), pp. 120–121.
20. Peter Beinart, *The Crisis of Zionism* (United Kingdom: Picador Publishing, 2013), p. 110.
21. For example, see Noah Pollack, "Peter Beinart and the Destruction of Liberal Zionism," *Commentary*, May 1, 2010.
22. Bret Stephens, "Israel Looks Beyond America," *Wall Street Journal*, February 15, 2016.
23. Jude Wanniski, "The Unanimous 9/11 Report," Lewrockwell.com, July 28, 2004.
24. Beinart, *The Crisis of Zionism*, p. 52.
25. Tribune News Service, "John Kerry Tears Into Israel Over Settlements on His Way Out the Door," *Chicago Tribune*, December 28, 2016.
26. Aron Heller, "Number of Arabs—'Accept Them or Not'—Now Nearly Equal to Jews in Holy Land, Demographer Says," *National Post*, March 27, 2018.

Chapter Five

Looking Ahead

Neoconservatism is now at a turning point. To borrow from the title of one of Norman Podhoretz's books, the country is now at a new "bloody crossroads" in its foreign policy. In the aftermath of the Iraq War, largely seen in public opinion and by elites as a great debacle, the public's acceptance of the neoconservative vision is currently at its lowest point. It is especially unpopular among the millennial youth. Offshore balancers, liberal internationalists, socialists, libertarians, and anti-globalist protectionists have far greater electability in the new political climate. Will neoconservatism survive? How will this movement's fate affect American-Israeli relations?

There are some positive signs, if not for neoconservatism but for America's continuing ties to Israel. The American public's support for the Jewish state against the two countries' common enemies does not appear to be in any danger of dissipating. Both Hillary Clinton and Donald Trump both proclaimed their commitment to the "special, unbreakable friendship" between the two countries. Trump told the crowd at the American Israel Public Affairs Committee (AIPAC) Policy Conference that he sees Israel as America' "cultural brother, the only democracy in the Middle East, the state of Israel."[1] Mrs. Clinton, likewise, declared at the 2016 AIPAC meeting that she believes in an "unwavering, unshakable commitment to our alliance and to Israel's future as a secure and democratic homeland for the Jewish people."[2] Both candidates have also pledged to reengage America in the Israeli-Palestinian peace process, with Trump asserting his corporate "deal making experience" as giving him the skills to be the president finally able to achieve it.

There is another positive sign. As Elliot Abrams has highlighted, Netanyahu's 2015 speech before Congress that the Obama administration and some Congressional Democrats boycotted was a success in the court of public opinion. In the Gallup Poll that followed, Americans' support for Israel rose from 49 percent to 53 percent.[3] The climb was across party lines, but support for Israel is still higher among Republicans. Not only did Bibi's support grow, it proved false the opinion of analysts that addressing Congress would be a mistake. Netanyahu's critics both in the United States and in Israel believed that his speech would hurt his country's relations with the United States and possibly even lose him his reelection against the Zionist Union leader, Isaac Herzog. Herzog said, "There is no doubt the prime minister knows how to speak well, but the truth is that the speech, as impressive as it was, did not prevent a nuclear Iran and won't impact a deal that is being drafted—not on its content, nor on its timetable." He continued: "The painful truth is that after all the applause, Netanyahu is alone and Israel is isolated, and the negotiations will continue without Israel's input. The speech sabotaged Israel's relations with the US. It will not change the view of the administration, only deepen the rift with our strategic ally."[4] But Netanyahu's speech did not isolate Israel from the United States. However, Herzog is right that the speech did nothing to prevent Iran's nuclear development, but Netanyahu probably did not expect that it would.

The decline of neoconservatism aside, support of Israel has surged in the Republican Party among both the leadership and the grass roots. Even while in 2016 Donald Trump's commitment to Israel has wavered a bit more away from the hardline than other candidates would have been permitted to get away with, it has now become something of a "litmus test" of any Republican presidential candidate's commitment to conservative American principles, of equal importance as opposing abortion and defending the right to bear arms. Trump, who, prior to being elected, was never seen as particularly strong on religious values or gun rights, has said that he would be a neutral broker on the Israeli-Palestinian conflict, if elected president. That is an exception, however. As Republican strategist Ron Bonjean has said:

> If you're a Republican and you hedge on your support on Israel, it's viewed as having a flawed foreign policy. It's a requirement for Republicans these days to be very strong on Israel if they're going to be taken seriously by primary voters. If you're not supporting Israel, then who are you supporting? Are you supporting Iran?[5]

While some of this is attributed to key Jewish donors to the party, most notably Sheldon Adelson, this new level of support for Israel cannot be thriving on that alone. For a party with such a low Jewish voter base, it cannot be possible without significant commitment from other key coalitions, especially Christian evangelicals. When in 2015, former Secretary of State James Baker delivered a speech at a J Street conference that was resolutely critical of Netanyahu, Governor Jeb Bush had to distance himself from his family's long association. Baker was a key foreign policy advisor for both his father and brother and was for decades one of the most respected Republican foreign policy experts. Even while his position on Israel's conflict with the Palestinians is the same now as it was in the 1990s, his perspectives on this single issue has more recently earned him a reputation of being less reliably conservative. Many neoconservatives, such as Jonathan Tobin, have long considered him a foe,[6] but the rest of Republican Party's respect for Baker has also diminished. As Bill Kristol put it, "Thankfully, James Baker doesn't speak for today's Republican Party."[7]

With the Republican nomination of Donald Trump for president, the most prominent neoconservatives were divided on which American political party is better for Israel in the 2016 election. Bill Kristol had stated on MSNBC in December 2016 after the Obama administration's abstention from the UN resolution vote on Israeli settlements that Trump would be much friendlier to Israel than the Obama administration and would "recalibrate" the relationship between the United States and Israel. But Kristol did not indicate if he believed a Hillary Clinton presidency would have continued and extended Obama's less favorable policies. Kristol and John Podhoretz stated that would be voting independent, most likely for Evan McMullin. Max Boot, Robert Kagan, Bret Stephens, and Joshua Muravchik all stated that they would go so far as to vote for Mrs. Clinton. Almost two years after Trump's election, and very soon after Trump announced America would recognize Jerusalem as Israel's capital, Stephens penned a piece in the *New York Times* stating why he is still a "Never Trumper." He said that despite his agreement with many of Trump's policies, "I still wish Hillary Clinton were president."[8]

There are two main reasons many of the neoconservatives opposed Trump's candidacy and went so far as to vote for other the Democrat candidate. The first is their antipathy to his vulgarity and lack of personal character. Stephens references Trump's "lying, narcissism, bullying, bigotry, crassness, name calling, ignorance, paranoia, incompetence and pettiness," and argues that it is profoundly non-conservative to support someone without basic decency and experience in public service for the office of the presidency.[9] Joshua Muravchik likewise has said that Trump has debased American politics to an unusual and aberrant level of indecency.[10] Max Boot said, "I'm literally losing sleep over Donald Trump. . . . I would hope that the party would fracture if the nominee were a fascist demagogue like Donald Trump."[11] Daniel Pipes wrote a litany of reasons for his decision to leave the Republican Party after Trump's nomination, citing that, "Supporting Trump translates into never again being able to criticize a Democrat on the basis of character."[12] Bill Kristol, who thinks Trump's political talents, while masterful, are exclusively demagogic, likened Trump's foray into politics to an episode in reality television.[13] Kristol also released a video compilation of

Trump expressing approving statements about Bashar Assad, Moammar Ghadafi, and Saddam Hussein.[14] John Podhoretz also said that Trump is "disgusting and nauseating."[15]

Robert Kagan had perhaps the harshest rebuke for then-candidate Trump and for the Republican Party that was about to nominate him for the presidency. Kagan thought Trump's ascendency in the Republican Party would be the beginning of a road to tyranny and fascism in the United States. In a *Washington Post* piece titled, "This is How Fascism Comes to America," he wrote:

> [Trump's] program, such as it is, consists chiefly of promises to get tough with foreigners and people of nonwhite complexion. . . . The phenomenon he has created and now leads has become something larger than him, and something far more dangerous. . . . Republican politicians marvel at how he has "tapped into" a hitherto unknown swath of the voting public. But what he has tapped into is what the founders most feared when they established the democratic republic: the popular passions unleashed, the "mobocracy." This phenomenon has arisen in other democratic and quasi-democratic countries over the past century, and it has generally been called "fascism."[16]

Kagan added that conservatives who dislike Trump's rhetoric and showmanship but think he can be tempered and molded into a good president once elected are "kidding themselves." He said, "What these people do not or will not see is that, once in power, Trump will owe them and their party nothing."[17] Kagan did not only vote for Hillary Clinton, he also helped fundraise for her by speaking at a "Hillary for America" fundraiser in Washington, DC. He even suggested that she is a neoconservative herself, by saying, "I feel comfortable with her on foreign policy. If she pursues a policy which we think she will pursue it's something that might have been called neocon."[18]

The second reason for neoconservative opposition to Trump's takeover of the Republican Party is the change in foreign policy they expected his isolationist populism would bring to the American Right. More fundamentally, though, they were concerned that Trump's lack of policy sophistication and his overly general campaign promise to "Make America Great Again" could not transform into a coherent foreign policy agenda. It was difficult, perhaps even impossible, to tell from Trump's rallies, speeches, and interviews, what exactly the "Trump Doctrine" would be on foreign policy. It was clear that he wanted the United States to strengthen southern border security, and that he vehemently opposed economic alliances like the North American Free Trade Agreement (NAFTA) and the Trans-Pacific Partnership. It was also clear that he supported the beefing up of America's military but in every place around the globe where America had a presence he either wanted to stop using America's military might to control geopolitical events or charge America's allies for their protection. He fervently criticized President George W. Bush and his neoconservative allies for bringing America into Iraq, yet offered no perspective on what America's Middle East policy should be. In fact, his entire argument for being the right person to lead the United States was his business acumen. He touted his talents in the "art of the deal," which he said he wanted to put to use in America's negotiations abroad. He said, "My whole life I've been greedy, greedy, greedy. I've grabbed all the money I could get. I'm so greedy. But now I want to be greedy for the United States. I want to grab all that money. I'm going to be greedy for the United States."[19]

When Trump spoke about the Israeli-Palestinian conflict, he suggested that his knack for making real estate deals would make him the president to finally broker a two-state arrangement. It seemed that he was going to be more sympathetic to the Israeli side than was President Obama. Despite some ridicule lodged at Trump's claim that a business background is useful for diplomacy, there is one person—an important diplomat—who does see merit in Trump's thinking like a businessman rather than as a diplomat. Michael Oren, Israel's former ambassador to the United States and deputy minister for diplomacy in Netanyahu's coalition, finds the business alternative to be more meaningful than the way of diplomacy. Oren encourages his government to accept Trump's peace proposal when it is announced. He argues that Trump, "unlike the previous president, views Israel as the solution and Iran as the problem." He says that it is unlikely that anyone else will ever offer a better deal than the president who is the most supportive of Israel's interests. Oren added, "In the world of business, if you leave the table you pay a price, you don't get rewarded. In the world of business negotiations, the first offer on the table is the best offer, the second offer is a less good offer, the third offer is less than that—just the opposite than in the world of diplomacy."[20]

In 1983, Trump received the "Tree of Life Award" for service to American-Israeli friendship from the Jewish National Fund. In several speeches throughout his 2016 campaign, he signaled support for Prime Minister Netanyahu, who had a very cold relationship with Obama. But there were still many unanswered questions as to what he would expect from Israel in his efforts to broker a peace agreement with the Palestinians. These questions emerged out of statements he made while running for president. In an interview with the *Associated Press*, Trump said, "A lot will have to do with Israel and whether or not Israel wants to make the deal—whether or not Israel's willing to sacrifice certain things."[21] At a Republican Jewish Coalition dinner, he continued to remain cryptic on what he expected of Israel when he said, "I don't know that Israel has the commitment to make it." His speech tapered from hot to cold with the staunchly pro-Israel audience when after receiving considerable applause, he was booed for being unwilling to say if the U.S. embassy should be moved to Jerusalem.[22] Throughout his 2016 campaign, there was a lot of mystery surrounding Trump's position on

Israel. *The Atlantic* inferred Trump's ambiguity on these issues as a "break with the GOP."[23] For many Jewish Republicans who supported him, however, his seeming neutrality on Israel did not ultimately derail their support for him. Ari Fleisher, former White House press secretary and a former spokesman for the Republican Jewish Coalition (RJC), said in March 2016, "As boorish as he is, as occasionally foolish as he is, and how vituperative he can be, I would vote for Donald Trump over Hillary Clinton any day."[24] However, for many neoconservatives, the lack of policy substance on this and many other issues was not really about whether or not Trump is committed to defending Israel's interests, but rather it suggested that he had a dangerous lack of knowledge about major international complications.

Although there is a tremendous difference between Donald Trump and Ronald Reagan, the neoconservatives were not particularly enthusiastic about the latter's candidacy in 1980 either, for some paralleled reasons. Irving Kristol, for example, found Reagan to be "vulgar."[25] E. Emmett Tyrell invited the Podhoretzes and the Kristols to a dinner he had arranged for Reagan and only the Podhoretzes came. And while the common thinking is that Reagan was the neoconservatives' perfect foreign policy president, actually nothing could be further from the truth. In 1982, Podhoretz penned a lengthy article in the *New York Times* titled, "The Neoconservative Anguish Over Reagan's Foreign Policy," in which he described Reagan's understanding of foreign affairs as "simplistic" but altogether "closer to the truth" than Carter's.

Norman Podhoretz, however, reluctantly endorsed Trump, as he also did for Ronald Reagan, whom he had some misgivings about. As Tyrell has stated about Podhoretz, "I recall Norman having his doubts about Reagan from time to time, for instance when the President sat down with Mikhail Gorbachev." But Podoretz supported Reagan over Carter in 1980, after backing Carter in 1976, because he considered him the lesser of two evils. Tyrell writes, "I say Norman and Midge made a 'calculation' because politics is usually a matter of calculating. Who, of the candidates in the field, comes closest to my ideal candidate?"[26] In 2016, while he viewed Trump as "impossible to predict," he believed that Clinton's participation in constructing the Iran agreement as secretary of state made her absolutely worse for Israel's interests. While a reluctant supporter of Trump, Podhoretz had always been "anti-anti-Trump," originally unwilling to bear the gravity of the neoconservative opposition to him when he was a candidate.[27] It is unclear, however, if his wife Midge Decter cast her vote for Trump too, but Tyrell, who knows the Podhoretzes well, indicated that he thinks she did.[28] Podhoretz says:

> I think there is no question that on Israel the Democrats can no longer be trusted. The liberal community, generally, and the Democratic Party, particu-

larly, have grown increasingly unfriendly to Israel over 50 years, and it's reached a point now where there are elements within the party who are positively hostile to Israel, and many who are simply cold and unfriendly.[29]

Jennifer Rubin, writing for the *Washington Post*, went so far as to say that the Obama administration is "the most anti-Israel in history."[30]

Although, according to a Pew Research poll, most Americans supported Israel over the Palestinians, there is less support for Israel among respondents who identify with the Democratic Party. 54 percent of Americans support Israel in the conflict and 19 percent support the Palestinians, while the numbers break down much more widely among Republicans, with 75 percent on the side of Israel, but among Democrats it is 43 percent for Israel and 29 percent for the Palestinians. Among supporters of Bernie Sanders, the "Berniecrats," who are the more liberal voting block in the Democratic Party, the number of supporters of Israel is even lower.[31] These polls were also taken before the shooting incidents of Palestinian terrorists and rioters along the Gaza border in April and May of 2018, in which there were some civilian casualties, and these events might have compromised even more Democrats' sympathy for Israel. If the Democratic Party moves further to the left with a more radical candidate in the mold of Sanders, Israel will have even less support from the Democrats than it did under President Obama.

Podhoretz knows, of course, the American Jews will never abandon their support for the Democratic Party on the basis of Israeli interests. He agrees with Abraham Foxman, the longtime president of the Anti-Defamation League (ADL), who in 2011 said that Israel has become a "wedge issue" between the two parties. Foxman lamented the decline of bipartisan support for the Jewish state and the "ugly tone" of rhetoric between the liberal and conservative wings of American politics on Israel.[32] But Foxman, the ADL, and the vast majority of American Jews, still vote for and support the Democratic Party. Among orthodox Jews there is a significantly higher level of independence from the Democrats, but it is still nearly half of the orthodox Jewish rabbinate that support them.[33] According to the Pew Poll conducted after the 2012 election, Jewish support for the Republican candidate did in fact grow by nine points since four years prior, but Mitt Romney still only received 30 percent of the Jewish vote that year.[34] In fact, Israel is a far more significant voting priority to evangelical Christians than to Jews. Tony Perkins of the Family Research Council, an evangelical lobby group and think tank, said, "Among core evangelical voters, Israel is easily one of the top 10, maybe even the top five issues when considering who to support in a presidential primary. The Old Testament tells us that whoever blesses Israel will be blessed and it's certainly important to be on the right side of God's word."[35] Whereas only 4 percent of American Jews rank Israel among their most important voting priorities.[36]

The reason Israel has become such a wedge issue between the two sides of the ideological spectrum is that the Left generally views politics in terms of a power dynamic between strong and weak. Leftist doctrines usually view the strong as the oppressive force and the weak as persecuted. Whether it is the rich exploiting the poor, or whites harming blacks with impunity, or men dominating women, or Christians in America persecuting non-Christians, the Left understands politics in terms of dominant classes possessing privilege over marginalized groups. The same scenario accounts for the Israeli-Palestinian conflict within a Leftist framework. Since the Israelis are obviously the stronger side in the struggle, it is they who should be withdrawing from their blockade of Gaza and making concessions of land for peace, rather than Hamas ceasing its terrorist activities. In regards to Israel's fears of a nuclear Iran, Leftists are more likely to blame Iran's nuclear ambitions on the fact that Israel threatens Iran with their own nuclear weapons, which the international community is not pressuring them to dismantle.

However, this is not the only reason for the Left's imbalanced criticism of Israel in Middle East politics or the wedge dividing the two parties. In addition to the Left's power dynamic framework, Leftists also do not see the contemporary world in terms of a "clash of civilizations." They do not think in terms of "western values" but rather in terms of "human rights." They disagree with conservatives that modern respect for liberty, democracy, freedom of religion, and the rights of women is a product of the West's Judeo-Christian tradition. Leftism refutes the conservative understanding of the world that assumes that non-Westerners, particularly those in the Muslim world, threaten the freedom and security that exists in America, Europe, and Israel. The phrase, "clash of civilizations," first coined by Bernard Lewis and popularized by Samuel Huntington, is deemed racist by the Left. The postmodernist intellectual, Edward Said, remarked of Huntington:

> Like Lewis, Huntington defines Islamic civilization reductively, as if what most matters about it is its supposed anti-Westernism. I mean it doesn't matter to him that Muslims have other things to do than to think about the West with hatred. But you get the impression that that's all they are thinking about is how to destroy the West, bomb it and destroy the whole world really.

Said also questioned the usefulness of the "clash of civilizations" model. He asked:

> Is it wise to produce a simplified map of the world and then hand it to generals and civilian lawmakers as a prescription for first comprehending and then acting in the world? Doesn't this in effect prolong and deepen conflict? What does it do to minimize civilizational conflict? Do we *want* the clash of civilizations? Doesn't it mobilize nationalist passions and therefore nationalist mur-

derousness? Shouldn't we be asking the question, why is one doing this sort of thing? To understand or to act? To mitigate or to aggravate the likelihood of conflict?[37]

Said's points encapsulate the Left's opposition to the neoconservative framework. It is the reason there is more sympathy within the Democratic Party for Iran and the Palestinians and harsher condemnations of Israel's behavior. Many on the Left, and in increasing numbers, do not see the Arab populations as being culturally more deficient of morals, nor Christians and Jews, as any more culturally decent. They believe that all cultures are equally capable of justice and all are equally capable of being inhumane. This understanding of all humanity as equally good and evil is a growing attitude within the ranks of the Democratic Party and has, for decades, been the general outlook among mainstream Western Europeans.

Conservatives, of course, see the world much differently. There are many variations of conservatism and each has its own foreign policy framework on what to do about defending the free world, but with a few exceptions, such as some paleoconservatives and libertarians, the wider "conservative movement" understands Israel as not only the sole beacon of Western values within a highly despotic region, but also as the West's first line of defense in the struggle against the Arab World. This is the reason neoconservatives emphasize Israel as much as they do. Podhoretz wrote:

> Most neo-conservatives would agree with Senator Moynihan's belief that the relentless ideological assault on Israel in the United Nations and elsewhere is more than a matter of calling the legitimacy of Israel itself into question; it also represents by extension a covert attack on the political culture of the United States and of the entire democratic world. In this perspective, the willingness to defend Israel (ideologically and politically no less than through military aid) becomes a subtle measure of our willingness to defend ourselves.[38]

But considering the fact that many of the prominent neoconservatives opposed Trump's nomination for his character defects, his demagoguery, and his lack of foreign policy sophistication, and that some of them even cast their votes for Hillary Clinton in 2016, it would seem that they are not single-dimensionally preferential to advancing Israel's security interests, as their critics ubiquitously claim. Just as this one policy issue does not chiefly motivate liberal American Jews, it does not singularly impel neoconservative Jews either. Putting aside Trump's occasional vagueness about Israel during his campaign, there is little question that Trump's outlook on Israel would make him the rational choice for neoconservatives if that were the singular issue that compels them over domestic and other foreign politics. Neoconservatives have long cataloged Clinton's anti-Israel activities and personal relationships. They have for many years considered her to be a political enemy, not a person they would prefer over a Republican candidate for president. One of the activities that was particularly egregious to them is when in 1999, as First Lady on a state visit to the Middle East, she sat and listened passively to Suha Arafat, the wife of Yasser Arafat, falsely allege that the Israeli military uses poisonous gas on the Palestinians, and then gave Arafat a hug. Upon criticism from figures in the American and Israeli media the following day, Clinton responded that Arafat's words were "inflammatory," but she did not denounce them as factually misleading.

Neoconservatives have also censured Clinton for many years for her friendship with and spiritual guidance from Michael Lerner. Lerner, who proclaims himself an ordained rabbi despite having never graduated from a Jewish seminary, was the founder and leader of the Seattle Liberation Front, a violent anti-Vietnam protest group in the 1970s, who has also criticized Israel at a level that Joshua Muravchik describes as "constant and invariably extreme."[39] Lerner started his magazine, *Tikkun*, to take "direct aim" at *Commentary*. According the Joseph Berger of the *New York Times*, who did a write-up on *Tikkun* when it first started in 1986, the magazine even parts ways with Jewish liberals in being concerned about anti-Semitism, but instead focuses on the experiences of "other oppressed minorities."[40]

More recently, after the leaking of Clinton's private emails, neoconservatives were particularly distraught by the anti-Israel advice she was getting from two of her closest advisors, Sidney Blumenthal and his son, Max Blumenthal. In his emails to Clinton, Sidney Blumenthal had told her that Israel is primarily responsible for the failure of the two sides to reach a peace settlement, and had particularly harsh words for Prime Minister Netanyahu as a ploy-artist, advising her to try to "catch" him. He also encouraged her to embrace J Street in order to marginalize the relevance of AIPAC, sent her an article by Jeremy Greenstock that argued that Hamas was a pro-peace organization, as well as a variety of other readings that were entirely imbalanced against the Jewish state.

In the early season of the 2016 election, during the time in which both parties were still in the nomination stage, Muravchik wrote a fairly long article in *Commentary*, titled, "Hillary Clinton's Bad Old Days," underscoring many of the parts of her history and personal alliances that made her, in his mind at the time, untrustworthy, particularly on matters related to Israel and the Middle East. Muravchik was particularly worried about her alliance with the Blumenthals. Max Blumenthal, he pointed out, is a common contributor to Mondoweiss, a fervently anti-Israel website edited by Ali Abunimah, the creator of the BDS movement. Blumenthal, Murachik noted, once wrote, "The extreme right [in Europe] is also attracted to Israel because the country represents its highest ideas . . . a racist and apartheid state." Murachik added that upon reading the article in which that line was contained, Clinton told Sidney that it is "A very smart piece." Murachik also added, "To another [article] that referred to 'the extensive history of Israeli and ultra-Zionist funding and promotion of Islamophobic propaganda in the United States,' [Clinton] commented, 'Your Max is a mitzvah.' To yet another that called the late Zionist blogger Rachel Adams 'an unabashed genocide enthusiast,' she blurted, 'Max strikes again!' The tone of goofy cheer indicates the level of solidarity and intimacy between Hillary Clinton and Sidney Blumenthal."[41]

Given all of this, the fact that so many of these prominent neoconservatives voted for Clinton over Trump ought to put to rest the idea that neoconservatives care more about Israel than America's interests. Their passionate disdain for President Trump suggests that what really motivates them is making America a defender of freedom and liberty both at home and throughout the world. Their "hard Wilsonian" hawkishness is about the expansion of American power to combat thuggish dictators, including, but not limited to, those in the Middle East, as well as Vladimir Putin and Kim Jong-Un. They do not see Trump as committed to American ideals and they worry about his failure to admonish them and his occasional tendency to praise them. Often alleged by their critics as fascist warmongers themselves, they are actually aggressively anti-fascism and promoters of using America's military arsenal to spread western democracy. Daniel Pipes, for example, implied that Trump would destroy the conservative movement's commitment to "a foreign policy reflecting American interests and values."[42] As Trump has, in the past, criticized neoconservative assumptions about what America's foreign policy ought to do, it does not matter to them that he has recognized Jerusalem as Israel's capital and canceled Joint Comprehensive Plan of Action on Iran, at the behest of Prime Minister Netanyahu, and that he has signed the Tyler Force Act, cutting funding to the Palestinian Authority.

Bret Stephens has said that Israeli officials informed him that they are seeking to broaden their spectrum of strategic partnerships.[43] As the Democratic Party has abandoned a lot of its previous friendly feelings toward Israel and with Trump's more protectionist stance regarding foreign military aid, Israel has come to the realization that it cannot count on the United States anymore as much as it has in recent decades. They are looking to form more strategic pacts with "aspiring start up nations" like India that want to emulate Israel's economic successes, and even with Islamic countries. Stephens thinks there is a strong basis for cooperation between Israel and Turkey, Saudi Arabia, and even Egypt. This would be a trend that both realists and liberal internationalists would be very happy to see continue. The neoconservatives do as well for Israel's sake, but they fear what the repercussions of this would have to American interests if the United States loses vital Israeli support. Israel will certainly always remain an ally of the United States, but there could be future moments in which the United States will find Israel unavailable and American requests unanswered. But neoconservatives should not look at it that way. Having greater independence from the United States is a good development for both countries' interests.

President Trump's envoys to Israel, David Friedman, Jason Greenblatt and Jared Kushner, have begun to promote stronger diplomatic relations between Israel and the surrounding Sunni Arab countries, in hopes that a better relationship between Israel and the outer Gulf Arab states would loosen those countries' knee-jerk support for Hamas as well cause pressure on Fatah to make substantial concessions at the bargaining table. It has been noted by Elliot Abrams that President Trump has reversed America's strategy of dealing with the Israeli-Palestinian conflict. He calls it the "outside-in" strategy. While all previous administrations, both Democrat and Republican have used the "inside-out" strategy, an attempt to broker peace with the Palestinians so that the tension with the rest of the Arab world is lessened.[44] The "inside-out" strategy has always been predicated on the assumption that Israel's problems with her neighbors are directly rooted in the statelessness of the Palestinian people. But the innovative approach of the Trump administration has been to turn the perceived dynamic on its head. Better relations with Saudi Arabia, for example, which already has covert ties based on mutual strategic interest over common threats from the Shiite regions of the Middle East, could finally lead to a brokered peace agreement between Israel and the Palestinian Authority.

As innovative as he thinks it is, Abrams, however, is very critical of the "outside-in" strategy. He believes that, just as conventional academic thinking has been for the last fifty years, this new approach also fails to see the hatred of Israel for what it really is. While he concedes that mutual interests do have the capacity to create temporary and covert cooperation between Israel and the Sunni countries, there are deeper-seeded hostilities that these Arab nations have for Israel and the Jewish people that cannot be resolved through overlapping interests. Nor are these Arab countries indifferent to the major sticking points of the Israeli-Palestinian disagreement. Abrams writes, "The covert relationship between Israel and the Gulf Arab states is highly fragile and might well be derailed should the negotiations bog down over such issues as Jerusalem and the 'right of return.'"[45] Most importantly, Abrams suggests, these Arab states actually do not even have enough influence over Palestinian leaders to create the pressure for concessions even if they wanted to. Similarly, Bret Stephens has said that Trump has been bad for Israel because what Israel needs, in his view, is what America has been since 1948, "an America committed to defending the liberal-international order against totalitarian enemies."[46]

Signifying a complete irrelevance of the neoconservatives in the post–Bush era in Washington, DC, Abrams was dropped from contention for Trump's deputy secretary of state. He has been a principal figure in the Reagan and Bush administrations, but having been very critical of Mr.

Trump during his campaign for president, Abrams was dropped from the list of contenders to serve in his State Department.[47] This was despite Abrams receiving strong support for the job from Rex Tillerson, Reince Priebus, and Kushner. But ultimately President Trump detests his critics, especially those who opposed him as strongly as Abrams did. In May 2016, at the point at which is was a foregone conclusion that Trump would be the Republican nominee, Abrams penned a *Weekly Standard* article, titled, "When You Can't Stand Your Candidate: A Story of 1972," comparing the Trump nomination to the 1972 Democratic Party nomination of George McGovern, which he thought was a comparable formula both for what he thought was the fecklessness of the new party direction and for the obvious "landslide defeat" in November he anticipated. Abrams did not recommend aligning with the "Never Trump" coalition, but he suggested the route taken by Scoop Jackson in 1972 of working toward stopping the nomination in every possible way but grudgingly supporting him once nothing further could be done to that end. "The party needs to be reminded that there are deep divisions," Abrams writes, "and Trump needs to be reminded of how many in the party oppose and even fear his nomination."[48] But, of course, Abrams' prediction of a landslide defeat never happened. Trump went on to win, unlike McGovern. Neoconservatives might be getting jobs on Trump's foreign policy team if they had not been so adversarial to his candidacy even against Hillary Clinton. And with more roles to play, the neoconservative view vis-à-vis Israel would be informing the administration's Middle East strategy.

As they look ahead, the neoconservatives can no longer rely on a unified Israel lobby. Not that it was ever entirely unified, but with the emergence of J Street as a fundamentally more liberal alternative to AIPAC, the neoconservatives face a more organized opposition to their approach. They do, however, appear to be holding their line quite adequately against the George Soros backed J Street. The new lobby organization has the strong disadvantage of having an agenda that is difficult to identify, whereas there is no question about what AIPAC and the neoconservatives have as their objectives. This seems to have hindered its effectiveness as a DC lobby. J Street's executive director Jeremy Ben-Ami blames his organization's problems on the "thuggish smear tactics" of the neocons, but in a political world that sees things in black and white, a group that is designed to add a shade of grey makes their overall mission suspect. One wonders if there is anything J Street agrees with AIPAC about, other than also claiming to support the Jewish state. As Ben Smith of *Politico* has put it about J Street:

> There's an odd contradiction in the group's posture: On one hand, they write of their growing influence in a pro-Israel universe dominated by hawks; on the other, they seem to suggest that there's no important distinction between their views and those of conservative Republicans or hawkish New Yorkers, when

on questions like Iran sanctions and engaging Hamas, J Street represents a more liberal line.[49]

But AIPAC is not the neoconservatives' Israel lobby. It is primarily an organization of Jewish liberals who just have a more hawkish approach to defending Israel than their fellow "New Left" Democrats. The neoconservatives' Israel lobby is the Emergency Committee for Israel (ECI). What makes the ECI different from the other Israel lobby organizations is its basic commitment to the status quo rather than transformative changes to Israel's policies. As Martin Kramer argues in a 2016 issue of *Foreign Affairs*, the ubiquitous perspective that Israel's status quo is unsustainable and that the Jewish state needs to take measures to create a roadmap to peace, is a misconception. Israel, Kramer argues, is sustaining its status quo just fine and has done so since the refounding in 1948. Kramer writes, "Israel's survival has always depended on its willingness to sustain the status quo that it has created, driving its adversaries to resignation—and compromise. This is more an art than a science, but such resolve has served Israel well over time."[50]

Pressure mounts within the Republican Party for cuts to, if not the total elimination of, foreign aid to Israel. Rand Paul, leading the GOP's libertarian wing, has made this case. Although Paul believes that cuts to foreign aid should begin with "countries that either hate us, burn our flag or persecute Christians or other religious minorities," his eventual goal is to eliminate aid to Israel as well. Libertarianism is growing increasingly popular as the national debt rises above $20 trillion. However, libertarians need to note that foreign aid contributes to roughly 1.4 percent of annual deficits, and the top three foreign aid recipients are Afghanistan, Iraq, and Israel.[51] Afghanistan and Iraq are countries the United States has invaded and are trying to prevent insurgent takeovers. Israel, on the other hand, is a strong ally and the United States supports it for a myriad other reasons. About Paul's proposal, Elliot Abrams said to the *Washington Post*:

> I have no doubt that some [foreign aid], especially under Obama, is wasted or misspent, but other parts constitute America's support for courageous people struggling to protect religious freedom and human rights in places from Cuba to Uzbekistan to Venezuela, to North Korea, Russia, and China.

Abrams adds:

> Those people are our natural allies and are fighting for what we believe in, and abandoning them is not only morally wrong but strategically dumb. They are risking life, limb, and prison to worship God freely and exercise their God-given rights. Should we really abandon them?[52]

Abrams' argument on behalf of foreign aid is a good example of why neoconservatives suffer so many public opinion defeats. In selling their policy priorities to the public, neoconservatives mostly emphasize America's moral obligations. Paleoconservatives like Paul Gottfried and Claes Ryn make an excellent point that they are no different from the Left in this regard. But one of the major reasons for the increasing appeal of libertarianism and Trump's nomination is that the public has grown tired of being told that they have a moral obligation to make sacrifices for other people. If neoconservatives would instead make their case by appealing to America's national *interest* instead of employing ideological abstractions and buzzwords like "honor," "national greatness" and "human rights," they would win a lot more fights in the battleground of public opinion than they do. How is it in America's interest to lend support to persecuted minorities in war-torn countries? How is it in America's interest to arm democratic governments to prevent their overthrow? And more specifically, how is Israel a vital American ally? Contrary to what they seem to think, the answers to these questions are *not* self-evident. Nor is a person immoral or un-American for failing to see the answers for themselves. Their failure to make a more reasoned case for public consumption is largely to blame for the caricature that neoconservatives are either disloyal Jews or jingoistic patriots.

If internal conflicts on the American Right are any indication, it is worth noting that Israel has not only been a wedge issue between the neocons and some paleocons, as previously discussed, the Israel issue has been a wedge in reverse on approval of President Trump. Pat Buchanan, of whom Joe Klein of the *New York Times* has called the "First Trumpist"[53] and one of the few long-time conservative columnists to have enthusiastically backed his candidacy, has expectedly been critical of Trump on the issue of Israel. After Obama's decision during his lame-duck session to have the United States abstain from the UN resolution on Israeli settlements, Trump tweeted, "Stay strong Israel, January 20 is fast approaching."[54] Buchanan reacted with a syndicated column expressing fears that President-elect Trump will weaken America's standing with all of the allies that voted in favor of the UN resolution, including Britain and France, as well weaken America's influence over Egypt, Jordan, and the Gulf Arab countries. He said, "Bibi's Israel First policy must one day collide with America First." Buchanan also referred to David Friedman, the appointed ambassador to Israel, as a "militant Zionist." He added that, "Politically, this will bring rewards in the U.S. Jewish community," and "once U.S. pressure ends and settlement building in the West Bank proceeds, Netanyahu, his hawkish Cabinet, the Israeli lobby, the neocons and the congressional Republicans will start beating the drums for Trump to terminate what he himself has called that 'horrible Iran deal.'"[55] Soon after the column was run, Bill Kristol tweeted, "Buchanan unhappy

[with] Trump being pro-Israel. Not the only issue on which I suspect Trump will break Pat's heart."[56]

Neoconservatives, on the other hand, do not see Trump as all that great for Israel. Bret Stephens in fact suggests that Trump really has not shifted away in any substantial sense from the Obama presidency on its Israeli policies.[57] Despite lip service, Stephens said in 2017, the Iran nuclear deal will not be scrapped as promised, the U.S. embassy will not be moved to Jerusalem, and the White House's official stance on settlement construction outside the Green Line security perimeter has not significantly changed with the incoming personnel. Rhetoric has changed in that Trump's May 2017 speech at the Israel Museum emphasized Israel's ancient connection to the Holy Land and called on Palestinians to stop funding terrorists and their families. It was a significant departure from Obama's Cairo speech, which was given at about the same stage in his first hundred days. But even rhetorically, Trump administration officials have been prone to gaffes, such as Secretary of State Rex Tillerson calling Tel Aviv, rather than Jerusalem, the "home of Judaism" and later, his refusal to say that the Western Wall is in Israel.[58]

But by 2018, Stephens turned out to be wrong. President Trump recognized Jerusalem, the embassy was indeed moved, and the Joint Comprehensive Plan of Action with Iran was canceled by the United States. Caroline Glick of the *Jerusalem Post* went so far as to call Trump the "most pro-Israel president in U.S. history." She added, "No other president comes close," and that, "The difference between Trump and his predecessors is that Trump accepts Israel on its own terms. He doesn't expect Israel to do anything to "earn" American support. So long as Israel is in America's corner, he respects the Jewish state as America's ally. Trump has earned all the credit for transforming the U.S.-Israel relationship into a full-blown strategic relationship."[59] For recognizing Jerusalem, the mayor of Kiryat Yam even went so far as to name a park after the 45th U.S. president, to honor him for taking the "brave and unprecedented step that none of his predecessors were willing to take."[60] Justice Minister Ayelet Shaked of Israel's right-wing Jewish Home party also remarked, "The Trump administration is turning out to be the most friendly administration to Israel ever."[61] Prominent neoconservatives, however, don't share that same judgment. They deem some of his pro-Israel decisions as akin to the broken clock being right twice a day. Following the announcement of the embassy move, Max Boot wrote:

> Israel is the only country in the world whose self-proclaimed capital—the place where its seat of government is located—is not widely recognized by the international community. Much as I oppose President Trump on many issues, he got this one right. My only complaint is that this move is more symbolic than substantive.[62]

Some of Trump's policy shifts came from key personnel changes. The hiring of John Bolton as national security advisor was a particularly paradigm-shifting change in the White House staff. Originally short-listed for the job as secretary of state, Bolton did not make it into Trump's cabinet, reportedly because the president-elect disapproved of Bolton's mustache.[63] But in 2018, with the shake-up in Trump's foreign policy inner circle, Bolton was tapped by Trump to replace H. R. McMaster as the national security advisor. Although Bolton's mustache came up again as a possible impediment to him getting this position too,[64] it is likely that President Trump felt that as a policy advisor rather than as a representative of the United States on the world stage, his mustache would not be an insurmountable problem. Trump's aesthetic tastes in his personnel's appearance aside, Bolton's ideological visions were distant from the kind of foreign policy he espoused as a candidate for president. Bolton was a stalwart supporter of the Iraq War, for instance, and a member of the George W. Bush administration, which Trump harshly denigrated. Trump thought that the neoconservatives had a "long history of failed policies and continued losses at war."[65] Bolton is a "fellow traveler" of neoconservatives, and this was not going to be a neoconservative administration.

It is also true, however, that one never knows with Trump if his opposition to people is based on genuine policy disagreement or personal vendetta. Elliot Abrams, for example, was also being considered for a job in the State Department until Trump saw Abrams' criticisms of him in his earlier writings.[66] Bolton, on the other hand, had never been hostile to Trump during his campaign, as so many neoconservatives were. Bolton has also been a staple on the Fox News Channel, and Trump has had a habit of tapping various personalities he sees on television to work in his administration, such as Sebastian Gorka and CNBC's Larry Kudlow. David Frum snidely called these Trump's "TV-cartoon favorites."[67] At the time that Michael Flynn was terminated as the very fleeting NSA, Bill Kristol even suggested that Bolton might be an acceptable replacement with "broad government experience."[68] Frum, however, referred to Bolton's appointment as "the strangest Trump surprise yet," because he campaigned as "the candidate of anti-interventionism."[69]

Bolton, a senior fellow at the American Enterprise Institute, a frequent contributor to *Commentary* and *The Weekly Standard*, one-time advisor to Senator Jesse Helms, and formerly the interim UN ambassador under President Bush under a temporary recess appointment, has been a long-time neoconservative favorite. Upon his appointment as Trump's NSA, some of the neoconservatives who had fiercely opposed Trump's election became more optimistic, albeit only slightly, about Trump's foreign policy. Bret Stephens, in particular, was pleased. Stephens said, "I think someone like Bolton is going to restrain the isolationist impulses that have been really at the heart of Trump's foreign policy thinking. Impulses, not ideology."[70] Elliot Abrams also applauded Bolton's appointment.[71] John Podhoretz also approved of

Bolton joining the White House but explicitly denied that he is a neoconservative, but rather a "conservative hawk."[72] But it is safe to say that the neoconservatives are a lot happier with Bolton advising the president on foreign policy than Steve Bannon.

However, some neoconservatives had the opposite reaction when Bolton was hired. Max Boot, who thoroughly dislikes him, wrote a vehement polemic against Bolton in the *Washington Post*, referring to him as a "zealot . . . who has a well-earned reputation as a wild man." Boot added that Bolton's "antipathy towards international treaties and organizations is legendary and goes well beyond that of ordinary conservatives."[73] David Frum was also not so ecstatic, saying that Bolton is "a man of strong and certain opinions, but not one adept at winning friends, convincing doubters, soothing opponents, cajoling foreign leaders, or governing bureaucracy."[74] Frum penned a piece in *The Atlantic*, suggesting that Trump's hire of Bolton confirms that given his threat to rain "fire and fury" on North Korea and his 2017 missile strikes on Syria, Trump's claim to be an isolationist and opponent of using military force has been a big sham. He wrote, "It now seems clear that what Trump rejected in Bush's foreign policy was not the use of force, but the application of force in service to *democratic ideals* [emphasis added]. That has been the teaching of John Bolton for decades. It's not a paradox that the two men have now come together."[75]

Bill Kristol was happy that Bolton signifies an opportunity to alter the course of Trump's foreign policy. But he agreed with John Podhoretz that Bolton was not altogether a neoconservative. In a *Weekly Standard* podcast, Kristol said:

> "He's not quite where I am and where most of the people at the *Weekly Standard* are on foreign policy, in the sense that he's less interested in democracy promotion abroad. He's more of a 'national interest first' kind of guy, a little closer to Trump in that respect, but not as far as Trump is on the 'America first' side." Kristol added, "John believes in a strong foreign policy, an internationalist foreign policy, to be fair, a strong believer in our alliances, a strong believer in our friendship with Israel."[76]

Not only is Bolton a stalwart supporter of the alliance with Israel, during his tenure as UN ambassador he frequently countermanded Condoleezza Rice, whose support for Israel was not so straightforward. On several occasions, he alerted Israel's UN ambassador, Dan Gillerman, to Rice's plans, when he thought they would jeopardize Israel's diplomatic hand. He also occasionally asked Gillerman to notify Prime Minister Ehud Olmert of the administration's plans to vote against Israel in the Security Council. For example, in 2006, the Security Council was ready to pass Resolution 1701, which called for a full cessation of hostilities between Israel and Lebanon. France was acting as the intermediary between the two sides and had been pushing the ceasefire, which had conditions that were, at the time, unacceptable to Israel. According to Gillerman, Bolton called him at 8 A.M. and told him, "Condi Rice sold you out to the French."[77] In her memoir, *No Higher Honor*, Rice recalls how Bolton went against her at the UN numerous times, especially when it related to Israel.

It was only shortly after Bolton joined the White House that Trump announced the cancellation of the Joint Comprehensive Plan of Action on Iran, the agreement President Obama made with Iran alongside several other countries, which dropped sanctions in exchange for a ten-year moratorium on nuclear weapons production. Conservatives have long been critical of Obama's pact with Iran, and neoconservatives have especially opposed it, fearing that the time period of ten years is not enough and that in addition to still allowing some uranium enrichment it still allows Iran's military bases to go unmonitored by inspectors. They do not believe Iran can be trusted and this is dangerous most especially to Israel and the upper hand Israel, the lone democracy in the region, has in the power dynamic of the Middle East. Trump's announcement that he is cancelling the agreement also came very soon after Prime Minister Netanyahu revealed to the world its newly acquired intelligence on Iran's nuclear program from 2003 to 2009. Whether Trump's decision was prompted by that or from the urging of his new national security advisor, Bolton, is unknown. It is most likely a combination of the two. Trump himself, even without these variables, has always been against Obama's Iran agreement, and most of what Netanyahu revealed was already known.

What is known, however, is that Bolton will be advising Trump what to do from here on out about Iran, now that Obama's agreement has been scrapped by the United States. It is safe to say that neoconservatives are much more comfortable with him at the helm within Trump's national security advisory circle during this phase than many other alternatives. Nevertheless, he is a controversial figure who is not even universally liked by Republicans. Some consider him to be something of a loose cannon and a "mean boss" who would not even pass confirmation in a Republican-controlled Senate.[78]

In 2009, after President Obama took office but before his speech in Cairo, Bolton authored an article in *Commentary* titled, "Israel's Diplomatic Isolation," looking ahead to the next four years and lamenting the way Israel is "always cast in the role of villain and for which matters are therefore certain to end unhappily."[79] Largely arguing his belief that the United Nations is a feckless institution, Bolton sympathizes with Israel's predicament as a pariah in the international community. Bolton is also a skeptic of the two-state solution. He once said, "I don't think there is a viable Palestinian state. I don't think there are institutions on the Palestinian side that can live up to the commitments of a treaty with Israel, that could give Israel or the United

States or anyone confidence that such a state could provide for the well-being of the Palestinian people or could resist takeover by terrorist elements."[80]

Israel's governing coalition was certainly pleased by Trump's decision to appoint Bolton. They know he was instrumental in getting President George H. W. Bush's State Department in 1991 to work toward rescinding the UN's 1975 "Zionism is Racism" resolution. His unwavering support of Israel is also reflected by the extent of the Palestinians' revulsion of him. Hanan Ashrawi of the Palestine Liberation Organization (PLO) said, "This man has a long history of hostility to Palestinians, dating to when he was at the United Nations, where he was protecting Israeli immunity," and added that in league with "extreme Zionists," he will "lead to a devastating reality for Palestine in the region."[81] Jeremy Ben-Ami of the J Street lobby also said of Bolton: "We are horrified by his selection to be national security adviser and believe this move by the president gravely imperils our country's national standing and the fundamental security of the United States and its allies, including Israel."[82]

Since being appointed secretary of state, Mike Pompeo has also said all the right things with respect to Israel that are sure to make neoconservatives happy. Unlike Bolton, he is not someone with whom the neoconservatives have had a close history, but he may be likely to forge a better appreciation from them than Rex Tillerson, his predecessor. On his first state visit to the Middle East, he joined Netanyahu in a press briefing and said, "We remain deeply concerned about Iran's dangerous escalation of threats to Israel and the region and Iran's ambition to dominate the Middle East remains. . . . The United States is with Israel in this fight."[83] As tensions along the Gaza border flared up and Israel faced international condemnation for killing Palestinian rioters lodging explosives and attempting to break through the barrier into Israel, Pompeo assured the Israelis that "We do believe the Israelis have the right to defend themselves, and we're fully supportive of that." He also expressed said, "We're certainly open to a two-party solution as a likely outcome. We certainly believe the Israelis and Palestinians need to have political engagement. We urge the Palestinians to return to that political dialogue."[84]

But the person in the Trump administration most lauded by neoconservatives in UN Ambassador Nikki Haley. Besides her reported tendency "to say too much too soon,"[85] the neoconservatives have been consistently pleased by her defense of Israel on the floor of the UN. She has given the UN members more than one earful about their bias against the Jewish state and western values. In January 2017, Haley said this on the floor of the UN: "Nowhere has the UN's failure been more consistent and more outrageous than its bias against our close ally Israel. . . . In the General Assembly session just completed, the UN adopted twenty resolutions against Israel and only six targeting the rest of the world's countries combined."[86] After the Gaza border incident on May 15, 2018 that resulted in nearly sixty Palestinian casualties, Haley also asked her UN Security Council colleagues, "Who among us would accept this type of activity on your border? No one would. No country in this chamber would act with more restraint than Israel has. In fact, the records of several countries here today suggest they would be much less restrained."[87]

Haley also defends against anti-Americanism at the UN. She said, "We contribute 22 percent of the U.N.'s budget, far more than any other country . . . but we must ask ourselves: What good is being accomplished by this disproportionate contribution? Are we getting what we pay for?"[88] In 2017, when the UN General Assembly was about to pass a resolution against the United States in response to Trump's recognition of Jerusalem as Israel's capital, Haley told the member nations that the United States will be "taking names" of the countries that vote for it and they may no longer be receiving foreign aid that the United States provides them. She has reminded them that under this administration, foreign aid is not a gift, but comes instead at a price.

Not all neoconservatives thought much of Haley's threat. Max Boot, the neoconservative who is perhaps the most critical and unforgiving of the Trump administration, described Haley's threat as "clumsy."[89] The problem, as he sees it, is that the administration has no intention of actually following through and withholding funds to any of those nations that voted for the resolution against the United States. Of course, hardly anyone really expected Trump to cut off their aid, although all bets are always off with this president, who never confines himself to the usual political guardrails. But even if he aid is not cut, it is possible to see Haley's threat as important posturing, to let them know that this administration is not going to be like its predecessor's in apologizing for America's sins rather than asserting America's strength. To that end, Haley's threat plays well to neoconservatism.

But to most neoconservatives, Haley stands fiercely for all the right principles, even when it is without depth. Daniela J. Greenbaum, in writing for *Commentary*, said that Haley is "one of the most reassuring features of the Trump administration."[90] Noah Rothman at *Commentary* also said that Haley's selection as UN ambassador indicates the incoming administration's "contempt for the prevailing diplomatic culture in Turtle Bay."[91] Bill Kristol even hinted on Twitter that he wanted to see Haley challenge Trump in the 2020 presidential primary. He even took a poll from readers on who she should tap as her running mate after defeating Trump for the nomination.[92] Of course, a Haley primary challenge to Trump is improbable. Trump may face a party challenger in the reelection primary, but it is unlikely to be from someone within his administration, especially not the former South Carolina governor and UN ambassador, who probably has eventually presidential ambitions of her own in the years ahead and would be better positioned for it with Trump's endorsement. It is difficult to ascertain if Kristol was even serious, as in his poll he did not list politicians as running mate contenders, but Ben Sasse, Jonah Goldberg, Tammie Jo Shults, and Mike Gallagher—all columnists or radio hosts. But given that he during the 2016 election, he promoted with earnest intent David French, a *Weekly Standard* and *National Review* writer, to run for president as an independent, he may not have been just flippant.

In fact, if she does have presidential ambitions, Nikki Haley may be just where she wants to be right now as UN ambassador. She knows that although the UN ambassadorship is not the most powerful or important foreign policy position in the administration, it certainly provides the greatest opportunity for grandstanding. In both parties, many prominent figures have developed their notorieties as UN ambassadors, often by delivering orations that make for newsworthy sound bites. There is no question that Haley is making the most of her position as America's representative to the UN. She is doing it in ways that play well to her party. Jonathan Tobin noted that as UN ambassador, Haley was in an especially unique position to steal thunder from her boss, the secretary of state, Rex Tillerson. Tobin writes, "Nikki Haley is speaking out frequently on issues such as human rights, Israel, Iran, and Syria in ways that make it clear that, like some of her predecessors, she understands that the U.N. post is the ideal bully pulpit."[93] Combined with her two terms as a governor, this experience may very well be more beneficial to her future than would a Cabinet-level position in the White House.

Haley may have to be vigilant, though, because she is working for a president who does not usually like to share the limelight. Haley is the one figure within the administration that did criticize his rhetoric during his presidential campaign, yet he still hired her. On international matters not directly related to the Israeli-Palestinian conflict, she parts ways with him on many humanitarian and moral matters. While he phoned Vladimir Putin of Russia and Recep Tayyip Erdogan of Turkey after their rigged election victories to congratulate them, and in China praised Xi Jinping's "permanent presidency," Haley has always been forthright in condemning illiberal governments. She told Bashar Assad, "The days of your arrogance and disregard of humanity are over," and even during her Senate confirmation hearing, she accused Russia of war crimes against the rebels in Syria.[94] Her statements against Russia have contradicted her president's, who has promised "warmer relations" with the Russian government. While she could be described as something of a neoconservative, the president clearly is not one. Max Boot, Trump's greatest neoconservative critic, has even called her the "conscience of the administration."[95] In fact, one wonders how much Haley and Trump actually align on most foreign policy matters. Regardless, however, the president seems to like her in her role. Early into his presidency, he told UN diplomats at a luncheon that Haley is "doing a fantastic job," but added, "She could easily be replaced."⁹⁶ It is possible that he likes her because she makes him look good, as she is the one part of his presidency that is unequivocally lauded by most members of her party and in the right-wing press.

At this point, even with Haley standing the Israel's ground at the UN and the embassy move to Jerusalem and the scrapping of the Iran nuclear agreement, the neoconservatives are far from convinced that the Trump administration is an effective guard for Israel's interests. Most of the more prominent neoconservatives do not agree with the public statements from some within Israel's right-wing parties and press that Trump is the more pro-Israel than any of his predecessors. Their primary concern is that not nearly enough is being done about Iran. They see not Iran's power grab in Syria as particularly the most existentially threatening concern for Israel. Max Boot has said, "Recognizing Jerusalem is the right thing to do. But if Trump truly wants to help Israel, he will focus more on curbing the Iranian threat—something that will be a lot harder to do, and carry greater risks, than simply issuing the kind of incendiary statements that he specializes in."⁹⁷

Looking ahead, the neoconservatives do not appear to be very politically well positioned anymore. While in the bastions of conservative journalism, the academy, and think tanks, neoconservatism still has an open-minded audience and a role to fill. In politics, there is a considerable backlash against them. At the present time, Trumpism has taken over the Republican Party, and while the populist, anti-elite fervor that swept Trump into victory in 2016 may be replaced in the long run, it does not seem evident that the kind of "hard Wilsonianism" neoconservatives stand for will widely embraced again any time soon. Spreading democracy overseas by force had its moment in the sun during the Bush years in the aftermath of 9/11, but ambivalence to the kind of self-sacrificial effort it takes to facilitate regime change was a direct cause of Trump's ascendency in the Republican Party. If the GOP, with its more hawkish grass roots grew tired of that, it is even less likely that neoconservatism can find a home in the Democratic Party, either. For all of Robert Kagan's insistence that Hillary Clinton would have been a better guardian of neoconservative foreign policy principles, her party is moving even further to the Left. Even if she wanted to take the United States on forceful human rights missions overseas, it is growing less feasible as a salient platform in the Democratic Party. As the old saying goes, "This is not your father's Democratic Party," and that adage rings more true today than it did twenty years ago. The Vietnam and Iraq wars have greatly softened the American people's resilience to war. Joshua Muravchik's suggestion that the United States must "give war a chance"⁹⁸ is not a very marketable solution to the problem of Iran's rogue regime.

On Israel, the Left's sympathy for the Palestinians has grown so much and the strongest ally the neoconservatives have are the evangelicals, who were Trump supporters of which the neocons have lost major political capital since the 2016 election. But it is likely that they can put another coalition together in the future as they coalesce around a more commonly agreeable presidential candidate. The likelihood of that is significantly greater than finding support from a candidate in the Democratic Party, which aside from its Jewish contributors and the AIPAC lobby, is fast moving toward conforming to the interpretation of Middle Eastern politics that Jimmy Carter, Edward Said, Noam Chomsky, and Norman Finkelstein have been propounding, which sees the Palestinians as the persecuted party and the Israelis the persecutors. AIPAC is no longer the sole Israel lobby. If it were as powerful as it once was, the United States would not have signed the Joint Comprehensive Plan of Action in 2015. The neoconservatives will have to adjust to a larger variety of lobbies on the Middle East. The Democratic Party once had greater unanimity on Israel, but it has become so much of a wedge issue among Democrats that Senate minority leader Charles Schumer, despite supporting the embassy move, refused to go to Jerusalem to attend the unveiling. Even for a New York politician like Schumer, there are too many political risks involved for Democrat politicians to go all in.

Israel's foreign policy is not based on democratization of its neighbors. Israel knows that it can forge peace with authoritarian regimes, as it did with Egypt and Jordan, and increasingly with Saudi Arabia and other Sunni gulf states that feel just as threatened by Iran and Syria as Israel does. Given the fact that the prospects of Republican presidencies get dimmer every election cycle because of the changing ideological demographics in the electoral map, the United States is not going to necessarily be there for Israel in the long run. Neoconservatives should therefore focus more on seeing Israel develop more friendships and alliances elsewhere, wherever possible.

The neocons have, perhaps, also an all-too rose-colored vision of the very American and Western civilization that they are trying to save. Much of the West is engulfed in its own self-guilt. The moral equivocation within the West's postmodern ethos makes it increasingly difficult to save the West from itself, much less from the barbarity of the illiberal world. It is unclear if this generation of neoconservatives understands this, but the first generation surely did. In 1968, Midge Decter wrote in *Harpers*, "At precisely a time when the values for which this community believes itself to stand—the enlargement of intellectual possibility and the devotion to standards of excellence—are being most threatened from the outside, it has responded only in kind, by threatening them further from the inside."[99]

The neoconservatives should therefore also reconsider the Jewish state's advantage as a "beacon of the West." The Declaration of the Establishment of the State of Israel promises that the Jewish state will be "based on freedom, justice and peace as envisaged by the prophets of Israel," and "will ensure complete equality of social and political rights to all its inhabitants irrespective of religion, race or sex." But that is not fully the basis of Israel's national purpose. It has a far deeper cause as the guardian of Jewish heritage and the security of the Jewish people. Not only do Israelis know this, they, for the most part, do not feel guilt for their own past. On the contrary, Israel is a society that widely cherishes the *simcha*, or the joy, of being Jewish, and the grand, long-awaited opportunity to live in their own homeland. It is founded not on an idea, or a set of principles, but on the heritage of a distinct people. In that regard, it is nothing like America.

NOTES

1. Donald Trump's speech to AIPAC, *Time*, March 21, 2016.
2. Hillary Clinton's speech to AIPAC, *Time*, March 21, 2016.
3. Elliot Abrams, "Gallup Votes for Bibi," *The Weekly Standard*, March 1, 2016.
4. Gil Stern Hoffman and Tovah Lazaroff, "Herzog: Netanyahu's Congress Speech Will Boomerang on Israel," *Jerusalem Post*, March 3, 2015.
5. Peter Baker, "For G.O.P., Support for Israel Becomes New Litmus Test," *New York Times*, March 27, 2015.
6. Jonathan Tobin, "Baker Creating J Street Challenge for Jeb," *Commentary*, March 20, 2015.
7. Ed O'Keefe, "Jeb Bush Stresses Support for Israel in Wake of James Baker's Comments," *Washington Post*, March 24, 2015.
8. Bret Stephens, "Why I'm Still a Never Trumper," *New York Times*, December 29, 2017.
9. Stephens, "Why I'm Still a Never Trumper."
10. Interview with Joshua Muravchik.
11. Zack Beauchamp, "One of the GOP's Biggest Hawks Explains Why He'd Vote for Clinton Over Trump," *Vox*, March 1, 2016.
12. Daniel Pipes, "Why I Just Quit the Republican Party," *Philadelphia Inquirer*, July 21, 2016.
13. *Real Clear Politics* Staff, "Bill Kristol: Donald Trump Knows 'Deep in His Heart' That He Should Never Be President," *Real Clear Politics*, September 23, 2016.
14. Ron Kampeas, "Prospect of Trump Nomination Poses Dilemma for Jewish Conservatives," *Times of Israel*, March 2, 2016.
15. John Podhoretz said this on MSNBC's "Morning Joe" on March 6, 2016.
16. Robert Kagan, "This is How Fascism Comes to America," *Washington Post*, May 18, 2016.
17. Ibid.
18. John Hudson, "Exclusive: Prominent GOP Neoconservative to Fundraise for Hillary Clinton," *Foreign Policy*, June 23, 2016.
19. Ezra Klein, "Trump: My Whole Life I've Been Greedy. . . . Now I Want to Be Greedy For the United States," *Vox*, January 29, 2016.
20. Aron Heller, "Michael Oren: Israel Should Welcome Trump Peace Plan," *Times of Israel*, May 1, 2018.
21. Brian Schaefer, "Where Does Donald Trump Stand on Israel?," *Ha'Aretz*, November 10, 2016.
22. Adam Chandler, "Donald Trump Breaks With GOP on Israel," *The Atlantic*, December 3, 2015.
23. Ibid.
24. Ron Kampeas, "Prospect of Trump Nomination Poses Dilemma For Jewish Republicans," *Times of Israel*, March 2, 2016.
25. R. Emmett Tyrell, "After Reagan Comes Trump," *The American Spectator*, September 14, 2016.
26. Ibid.
27. Lee Smith, "Norman Podhoretz, 89 Today, Has Made It," *Tablet,* January 16, 2019.

28. Ibid.

29. Eric Cortelessa, "Norman Podhoretz, the Last Remaining 'Anti-Anti-Trump' Neoconservative," *The Times of Israel*, September 7, 2016.

30. Jennifer Rubin, "Why It's Correct to Label the Obama Administration 'anti-Israel,'" *Washington Post*, January 20, 2016.

31. Jonathan S. Tobin, "Hillary vs. Liberals on BDS," *Commentary*, May 10, 2016.

32. Joel Brinkly, "Israel Becomes a Wedge Issue," *Politico*, December 15, 2011.

33. Kevin Quealy, "Your Rabbi? Probably a Democrat. Your Baptist Pastor? Probably a Republican. Your Priest? Who Knows," *New York Times*, June 12, 2017. Quealy discusses a study by Eitan D. Hersh and Gabrielle Malina. According to their data set, more than 40 percent of orthodox rabbis support the Democratic Party.

34. Pew Poll, "How the Faithful Voted: 2012 Preliminary Analysis," November 7, 2012.

35. Paul Stanley, "Where is Israel on Evangelical Christian Voters' List of Priorities?," *Jewish News Service* (JNS.org), August 27, 2015.

36. Daniel Cox and Robert P. Jones, "Chosen for What? Jewish Values in 2012," PRRI (http://www.prri.org/research/jewish-values-in-2012/).

37. Edward Said, "The Myth of the 'Clash of Civilizations,'" transcript from the Media Education Foundation, 1998 (https://www.mediaed.org/transcripts/Edward-Said-The-Myth-of-Clash-Civilizations-Transcript.pdf).

38. Norman Podhoretz, "The Neoconservative Anguish Over Reagan's Foreign Policy," *New York Times*, May 2, 1982.

39. Joshua Muravchik, "Hillary Clinton's Bad Old Days," *Commentary*, March 17, 2016.

40. Joseph Berger, "New Liberal Jewish Magazine Aims Fire at *Commentary* And Stirs Internal Protests," *New York Times*, October 26, 1986.

41. Ibid.

42. Daniel Pipes, "Why I Just Quit the Republican Party," *Philadelphia Inquirer*, July 21, 2016.

43. Bret Stephens, "Israel Looks Beyond America," *Wall Street Journal*, February 15, 2016.

44. Elliot Abrams, "U.S.-Israel Relations in the Trump Era," *Middle East Forum*, June 15, 2017.

45. Ibid.

46. Bret Stephens, "Donald Trump is Bad for Israel," *The New York Times*, December 26, 2018.

47. Jamie Gangel and Elise Labott, "Trump Nixes Elliot Abrams for State Department Job," *CNN*, February 10, 2017.

48. Elliot Abrams, "When You Can't Stand Your Candidate: A Story of 1972," *The Weekly Standard*, May 16, 2017.

49. Ben Smith, "J Street Blames 'Neocons' . . . 'Thuggish Smear Tactics' for Conference Woes," *Politico*, October 16, 2009.

50. Martin Kramer, "Israel and the Post-American Middle East: Why the Status Quo is Sustainable," *Foreign Affairs*, July/August 2016, p. 53.

51. Jennifer Rubin, "Cut Off All Foreign Aid? That Would Be 'Dumb' and Dangerous," *Washington Post*, October 16, 2014.

52. Ibid.

53. Joe Klein, "Pat Buchanan Reveals Himself to Be the First Trumpist," *New York Times*, May 8, 2017.

54. Barak Ravid, "Trump: Stay Strong Israel, January 20th is Fast Approaching," *Haaretz*, December 28, 2016.

55. Patrick J. Buchanan, "Israel First, or America First?" *World Net Daily*, December 29, 2016.

56. Bill Kristol, 2:53 P.M., December 31, 2016. Twitter.

57. Jackie, Headapohl, "WSJ Columnist Bret Stephens Weighs in on Israel, the Media, Trump and More," *The Jewish News*, April 13, 2017.

58. Amir Tibon, "Trump's Secretary of State Refuses to Say Western Wall is in Israel," *Haaretz*, May 22, 2017.

59. Caroline Glick, "Column One: Netanyahu's Finest Hour," *Jerusalem Post*, May 10, 2018.
60. *Times of Israel* Staff, "Northern Israeli City to Name New Park After Trump," *Times of Israel*, December 7, 2017.
61. Jack Moore, "Trump Security Pick John Bolton Welcomed By Israelis, Reviled By Palestinians," *Newsweek*, March 23, 2018.
62. Max Boot, "Trump is Right About Jerusalem, But That's Not the Help Israel Needs," *Los Angeles Times*, December 22, 2017.
63. Philip Rucker and Karen Tumulty, "Donald Trump is Holding a Government Casting Call. He's Seeking 'The Look,'" *Washington Post*, December 22, 2016.
64. Josh Delk, "Officials Say Trump Was Hesitant in Hiring Bolton Because of His Mustache," *The Hill*, March 23, 2018.
65. Mark Mazetti, Helene Cooper, and Eric Schmitt, "'Never Trump' Becomes 'Maybe Trump' in Foreign Policy Sphere," *New York Times*, November 10, 2016.
66. Anne Gearan, "Trump Rejects Veteran GOP Foreign Policy Aide Elliot Abrams for State Dept. Job," *Washington Post*, February 10, 2017.
67. David Frum, "What Trump's Choice of Bolton Reveals," *The Atlantic*, March 23, 2018.
68. Bill Kristol, February 14, 2017 at 5:03 A.M. Twitter. Kristol said, "For what it's worth, I'd say what's needed is broad government experience. They won't (presumably) take Abrams. How about John Bolton?"
69. David Frum, "What Trump's Choice of Bolton Reveals," *The Atlantic*, March 23, 2018.
70. Joe Concha, "NYT's Bret Stephens: Bolton Will Restrain Trump's 'Isolationist Impulses," *The Hill*, March 28, 2018.
71. Eliana Johnson, "John Bolton's Knife-Fighting Skills Alarm His Critics," *Politico*, March 28, 2018.
72. Tweet from John Podhoretz, March 22, 2018 at 3:32 P.M. Podhoretz said, "John Bolton is a longtime friend and contributor to @Commentary. He is not, however, a neoconservative. He's a conservative full stop. Goldwater '64. But if you ask him who the best Secretary of State was in our time, he'll tell you it was James Baker. He's an interesting man."
73. Max Boot, "Add Another Zealot to the White House," *Washington Post*, March 22, 2018.
74. David Frum, "What Trump's Choice of Bolton Reveals," *The Atlantic*, March 23, 2018.
75. Ibid.
76. Podcast Interview with Bill Kristol: "John Bolton and the Uncertain Future of U.S. Foreign Policy, *The Weekly Standard*, March 23, 2018 (https://www.weeklystandard.com/tws-podcast/john-bolton-and-the-uncertain-future-of-us-foreign-policy).
77. Noga Tarniopolsky, "John Bolton Told Israel: Condi Rice Sold You Out; Ex-Official Says," *The Daily Beast*, March 27, 2018.
78. Senator George Voinovich said, "'I worry that Mr. Bolton could make it more difficult for us to achieve the important U.N. reforms needed to restore the strength of the institution." See NBC News, "Republican Asks Senators to Reject Bolton," *NBC News*, May 24, 2005 (http://www.nbcnews.com/id/7969246/ns/politics/t/republican-asks-senators-reject-bolton/#.Wv8LoC_My8U).
79. John Bolton, "Israel's Diplomatic Isolation," *Commentary*, May 1, 2009.
80. Jewish Telegraph Agency, "8 Reasons Why John Bolton Appointment is Causing a Frenzy Among Jews," *Jerusalem Post*, March 24, 2018.
81. Jack Moore, "Trump Security Pick John Bolton Welcomes By Israelis, Reviled By Palestinians," *Newsweek*, March 23, 2018.
82. Jewish Telegraph Agency, "8 Reasons Why John Bolton Appointment is Causing a Frenzy Among Jews," March 23, 2018.
83. Matthew Lee, "Mike Pompeo Takes a Tough Line On Iran During His First Trip Abroad as Secretary of State," *Time*, April 30, 2018.
84. Gardiner Harris, "Mike Pompeo Expresses Support For Israeli Response to Gaza Protests," *New York Times*, April 30, 2018.
85. Editors, "A Failure to Communicate," *The Weekly Standard*, April 20, 2018.

86. Jenna Lifhits, "Haley Slams Anti-Israel Bias at the United Nations, *The Weekly Standard*, January 18, 2017.

87. Tovah Lazaroff and Daniel J. Roth, "Haley Says Hamas Pleased By Deaths; PA Envoy Calls Her a Racist," *Jerusalem Post*, May 16, 2018.

88. Jenna Lifhits, "Haley Slams Anti-Israel Bias at the United Nations," *The Weekly Standard*, January 18, 2017.

89. Max Boot, "Trump is Right About Jerusalem, But That's Not the Help Israel Needs," *Los Angeles Times*, December 22, 2017.

90. Daniela J. Greenbaum, "Nikki Haley: A Diplomat Who Delivers," *Commentary*, December 18, 2017.

91. Noah Rothman, "A Proper Contempt for the UN," *Commentary*, November 23, 2016.

92. Bill Kristol, 2:11 P.M., December 10, 2017. Twitter. "The Nikki Haley primary challenge to Trump in 2020 is going to be epic"; Bill Kristol, 19 April 2018, Twitter, "After Nikki Haley defeats Trump for the GOP nomination in 2020, whom should she pick as her running mate?"

93. Jonathan S. Tobin, "Is Nikki Haley the Alternative Secretary of State?" *National Review*, June 30, 2017.

94. Vivian Salama, "Nikki Haley Remains Boldly Off-Message at the UN," *Times of Israel*, May 1, 2017.

95. Max Boot, "The Conscience of an Administration," *Commentary*, April 20, 2017.

96. Ibid.

97. Max Boot, "Trump is Right About Jerusalem, But That's Not the Help Israel Needs."

98. Joshua Muravchik, "War is the Only Way to Stop Iran," *Washington Post*, March 15, 2015.

99. Midge Decter, "Anti-Americanism in America," *Harpers*, April 1968.

Bibliography

Abrams, Elliot. "When You Can't Stand Your Candidate: A Story of 1972," *The Weekly Standard*, May 16, 2017.
Alpher, Yossi. "Sharon Warned Bush," *Forward*, January 12, 2007.
Arthur Hertzberg. *The Zionist Idea*. New York: The Jewish Publication Society, 1997.
Arutz Sheva Staff. "Satmar Rebbe: 'Tear Your Garment' Over Netanyahu," *Arutz Sheva*, May 22, 2018.
Associated Press. "Rice: 'It's Time' for a Palestinian State," *NBC News*, October 15, 2007.
Balint, Benjamin. *Running Commentary*. New York: Public Affairs, 2011.
BBC News Staff. "Palestinians Get Saddam Funds," *BBC News*, March 13, 2003.
Beauchamp, Zack. "One of the GOP's Biggest Hawks Explains Why He'd Vote for Clinton Over Trump," *Vox*, March 1, 2016.
Beinart, Peter. *The Crisis of Zionism*. United Kingdom: Picador Publishing, 2013.
Benhorin, Yitzhak. "Israel Warned Us Against Iraq Invasion, U.S. Official Says," *Yedioth Ahronot*, September 1, 2007.
Benn, Aluf. "What's the Hurry," *Ha'Aretz*, December 27, 2007.
Berger, Joseph. "New Liberal Jewish Magazine Aims Fire at *Commentary* and Stirs Internal Protests," *New York Times*, October 26, 1986.
Berman, Lazar. "Iran Militia Chief: Destroying Israel is Nonnegotiable," *Times of Israel*, March 31, 2015.
Boehm, Omri. "Liberal Zionism in the Age of Trump," *New York Times*, December 20, 2016.
Bolton John. "Israel's Diplomatic Isolation," *Commentary*, May 1, 2009.
Boot, Max. "Add Another Zealot to the White House," *Washington Post*, March 22, 2018.
Boot, Max. "Myths About Neoconservatism," *The Neocon Reader*, ed. Irwin Stelzer. New York: Grove Press, 2004.
Boot, Max. "The Conscience of an Administration," *Commentary*, April 20, 2017.
Boot, Max. "Trump is Right About Jerusalem, But That's Not the Help Israel Needs," *Los Angeles Times*, December 22, 2017.
Breitbart TV. "Kristol Responds to 'Renegade Jew' Article: 'I'm a Proud Jew, Strong Supporter of Israel," *Breitbart*, May 17, 2016.
Buchanan, Patrick J. "Israel First, or America First?" *World Net Daily*, December 29, 2016.
Buchanan, Patrick J. "On to Damascus?" *World Net Daily*, April 9, 2003.
Buchanan, Patrick J. "Resist the War Party on Crimea," *The American Conservative*, March 4, 2014.
Buchanan, Patrick J. "The Persecution of John Demjanjuk," *Townhall*, May 13, 2011.
Buchanan, Patrick J. "Zionism's Dead End," antiwar.com, June 28, 2008.
Buchanan, Patrick J. *A Republic, Not an Empire*. New York: Regnery, 2002.

Buchanan, Patrick J. *State of Emergency*. New York: St. Martin's Griffin, 2007.
Buchanan, Patrick J. *The Death of the West: How Dying Populations and Immigrant Invasions Imperil Our Country and Civilization*. New York: St. Martin's Griffin, 2002.
Buchanan, Patrick J. *Where the Right Went Wrong*. New York: St. Martin's Griffin, 1995.
Buckley, William F. *In Search of Anti-Semitism*. New York: Continuum International Publishing Group, 1992.
Bumiller, Elisabeth. "Rice's Turnabout in Mideast Talks," *New York Times*, November 26, 2007.
Carter, Jimmy. "The Elders' View of the Middle East," *Washington Post*, September 6, 2009.
Chandler, Adam. "Donald Trump Breaks with GOP on Israel," *The Atlantic*, December 3, 2015.
Concha, Joe. "NYT's Bret Stephens: Bolton Will Restrain Trump's 'Isolationist Impulses,'" *The Hill*, March 28, 2018.
Cortelessa, Eric. "Norman Podhoretz, the Last Remaining 'Anti-Anti-Trump' Neoconservative," *The Times of Israel*, September 7, 2016.
Coulter, Ann. *Adios, America: The Left's Plan to Turn Our Country into a Third World Hell-Hole*. New York: Regnery Press, 2015.
Cox, Daniel and Robert P. Jones. "Chosen for What? Jewish Values in 2012," PRRI. http://www.prri.org/research/jewish-values-in-2012/.
de Borchgrave, Arnaud "A Bush-Sharon Doctrine?" *Washington Times*, February 14, 2003.
Decter, Midge. "Anti-Americanism in America," *Harpers*, April 1968.
Decter, Midge. "Lone Wolf: A Biography of Vladimir (Ze'ev) Jabotinsky by Shmuel Katz," *Commentary*, July 1, 1996.
Decter, Midge. "The U.N. and U.S. National Interests," *Always Right: Selected Writings of Midge Decter*. Washington, DC: The Heritage Foundation, 2002.
Delk, Josh. "Officials Say Trump Was Hesitant in Hiring Bolton Because of His Mustache," *The Hill*, March 23, 2018.
Dougherty, Michael Brendan. "I Will Miss Joe Sobran," *The American Conservative*, October 1, 2010.
Editors. "A Failure to Communicate," *The Weekly Standard*, April 20, 2018.
Editors. "About" section of *The National Interest*. http://nationalinterest.org/about-the-national-interest.
Editors. "The Year That Conservatism Turned Ugly," *First Things*, May 1992.
Feith, Douglas. "For the Record—The 'Clean Break' Paper," DougFeith.com.
Fendel, Hillel. "Krauthammer on PA State, Obama, Pollard, and More," *Arutz Sheva*, August 8, 2010.
Findlay, Paul, forward to Stephen J. Sniegoski, *The Transparent Cabal: The Neoconservative Agenda in the Middle East, and the National Interest of Israel*. Virginia: Enigma Editions, 2008.
Francis, Samuel. *James Burnham: Thinkers of Our Time*. United Kingdom: Claridge Press, 1999.
Frum, David. "What Trump's Choice of Bolton Reveals," *The Atlantic*, March 23, 2018.
Frum, David. *Dead Right*. New York: Basic Books, 1995.
Gangel, Jamie and Elise Labott. "Trump Nixes Elliot Abrams for State Department Job," *CNN*, February 10, 2017.
Gearan, Anne. "Trump Rejects Veteran GOP Foreign Policy Aide Elliot Abrams for State Dept. Job," *Washington Post*, February 10, 2017.
Gershman, Carl. "The Andrew Young Affair," *Commentary*, November 1, 1979.
Glazer, Nathan. "The Enmity Within," *New York Times Book Review*, September 27, 1992.
Glick, Caroline. "Column One: Netanyahu's Finest Hour," *Jerusalem Post*, May 10, 2018.
Goldberg, Jeffrey. "The Neocons Split with Israel Over Egypt," *The Atlantic*, February 2, 2011.
Goldberg, Michelle. "Breitbart Calls Trump Foe 'Renegade Jew.' This is How Anti-Semitism Goes Mainstream," *Slate*, May 16, 2016.
Gordon, Evelyn. "Provocation at the Wall," *Commentary*, September 1, 2013.
Gottfried, Paul E. *Leo Strauss and the Conservative Movement in America*. United Kingdom: Cambridge University Press, 2011.

Gottfried, Paul E. *War and Democracy*. Hungary: Arktos Media Limited, 2012.
Greenbaum, Daniela J. "Nikki Haley: A Diplomat Who Delivers," *Commentary*, December 18, 2017.
Harris, Gardiner. "Mike Pompeo Expresses Support for Israeli Response to Gaza Protests," *New York Times*, April 30, 2018.
Headapohl, Jackie. "WSJ Columnist Bret Stephens Weighs in on Israel, the Media, Trump and More," *The Jewish News*, April 13, 2017.
Heilbrunn, Jacob. *They Knew They Were Right*. New York: Doubleday, 2008.
Heller, Aron. "Michael Oren: Israel Should Welcome Trump Peace Plan," *Times of Israel*, May 1, 2018.
Heller, Aron. "Number of Arabs—'Accept Them or Not'—Now Nearly Equal to Jews in Holy Land, Demographer Says," *National Post*, March 27, 2018.
Herman, Arthur. "Will Israel Be the Next Energy Superpower?" *Commentary*, March 1, 2014.
Horowitz, David. "Bill Kristol: Republican Spoiler, Renegade Jew?" in *Breitbart*, May 15, 2016.
Hudson, John. "Exclusive: Prominent GOP Neoconservative to Fundraise for Hillary Clinton," *Foreign Policy*, June 23, 2016.
Information Clearing House. "A Clean Break: A New Strategy for Securing the Realm," http://www.informationclearinghouse.info/article1438.htm), July 10, 2018.
Jewish Telegraph Agency. "8 Reasons Why John Bolton Appointment is Causing a Frenzy Among Jews," *Jerusalem Post*, March 24, 2018.
Johnson, Eliana. "John Bolton's Knife-Fighting Skills Alarm His Critics," *Politico*, March 28, 2018.
Kagan, Robert. "American Power—A Guide for the Perplexed," *Commentary*, April 1996.
Kagan, Robert. "This is How Fascism Comes to America," *Washington Post*, May 18, 2016.
Kampeas, Ron. "Prospect of Trump Nomination Poses Dilemma for Jewish Conservatives," *Times of Israel*, March 2, 2016.
Kaplan, Fred. "Why Israel, Saudi Arabia, and Neocons Hate the Iran Deal," *Slate*, July 14, 2015.
Karta, Neturei. "Judaism and Zionism Are Not the Same Thing," Nkusa.org. http://www.nkusa.org/AboutUs/Zionism/judaism_isnot_zionism.cfm.
Kirk, Russell. "Neoconservatism: An Endangered Species," Heritage.org. http://www.heritage.org/research/lecture/the-neoconservatives-an-endangered-species.
Klein, Ezra. "Trump: My Whole Life I've Been Greedy . . . Now I Want to Be Greedy for the United States," *Vox*, January 29, 2016.
Klein, Joe. "Pat Buchanan Reveals Himself to Be the First Trumpist," *New York Times*, May 8, 2017.
Kramer, Martin. "Israel and the Post-American Middle East: Why the Status Quo is Sustainable," *Foreign Affairs*, July/August 2016, p. 53.
Krauthammer, Charles. "At Last, Zion," *The Weekly Standard*, May 11, 1998.
Krauthammer, Charles. *Things That Matter*. New York: Crown Forum, 2003.
Krieger, Zvika. "What Condi Rice's Memoir Gets Wrong (and Right) on Israel," *The Atlantic*, October 27, 2011.
Kristol, Bill. 2:11 P.M., December 10, 2017, Twitter.
Kristol, Bill. 2:53 P.M., December 31, 2016, Twitter.
Kristol, Bill. 5:03 A.M., February 14, 2017, Twitter.
Kristol, Bill. "John Bolton and the Uncertain Future of U.S. Foreign Policy," *The Weekly Standard* Podcast, March 23, 2018. https://www.weeklystandard.com/tws-podcast/john-bolton-and-the-uncertain-future-of-us-foreign-policy.
Kristol, Bill, unknown time, April 19, 2018, Twitter.
Kristol, Irving. "A Conservative Welfare State," *The Wall Street Journal*, June 14, 1993.
Kristol, Irving. "Kissinger at a Dead End," *The Wall Street Journal*, March 10, 1976.
Kristol, Irving. "The Future of American Jewry," in *Neoconservatism: An Autobiography of an Idea*. New York: The Free Press, 1995.
Kristol, Irving. *Reflections of a Neoconservative*. New York: Basic Books, 1983.

Kristol, William and Robert Kagan. "Saddam Must Go," *The Weekly Standard*, November 17, 1997.
Kristol, William. "Speaking for Israel—And America," *The Weekly Standard*, March 16, 2015.
Lazaroff, Tovah and Daniel J. Roth. "Haley Says Hamas Pleased by Deaths; PA Envoy Calls Her a Racist," *Jerusalem Post*, May 16, 2018.
Lee, Matthew. "Mike Pompeo Takes a Tough Line on Iran During His First Trip Abroad as Secretary of State," *Time*, April 30, 2018.
Lewis, Anthony J. "Israel's Censorship Would Gall Brandeis," *The Spokesman Review*, May 21, 1982.
Lifhits, Jenna. "Haley Slams Anti-Israel Bias at the United Nations," *The Weekly Standard*, January 18, 2017.
Mazetti, Mark Helene Cooper, and Eric Schmitt. "'Never Trump' Becomes 'Maybe Trump' in Foreign Policy Sphere," *New York Times*, November 10, 2016.
McConnell, Scott. "I Like and Respect Israel—But It's Not America," *The American Conservative*, September 26, 2012.
Mearsheimer, John and Stephen Walt. "The Israel Lobby," *London Review of Books*, Vol. 28, No. 6, March 23, 2006.
Moore, Jack. "Trump Security Pick John Bolton Welcomed by Israelis, Reviled by Palestinians," *Newsweek*, March 23, 2018.
Mozgovaya, Natasha. "Obama Camp Dismisses Jesse Jackson's Israel Policy Remarks," *Ha'aretz*, October 14, 2008.
Muravchik, Joshua. "Facing Up to Black Anti-Semitism," *Commentary*, December 1, 1995.
Muravchik, Joshua. "Here's How the World Turned Against Israel," *The Weekly Standard*, December 2, 2014.
Muravchik, Joshua. "Hillary Clinton's Bad Old Days," *Commentary*, March 17, 2016.
Muravchik, Joshua. "John Demjanjuk: A Summing Up," *Commentary*, April 1, 1997.
Muravchik, Joshua. "Our Worst Ex-President," *Commentary*, February 2007.
Muravchik, Joshua. "Pat Buchanan and the Jews," *Commentary*, January 1991.
Muravchik, Joshua. "War is the Only Way to Stop Iran," *Washington Post*, March 15, 2015.
Muravchik, Joshua. *Exporting Democracy*. Washington, DC: American Enterprise Institute Press, 1992),.
Muravchik, Joshua. *Making David Into Goliath*. New York: Encounter Books, 2014.
Muravchik, Joshua. *The Imperative of American Leadership*. Washington, DC: American Enterprise Institute, 1996.
NBC News. "Republican Asks Senators to Reject Bolton," *NBC News*, May 24, 2005.
Nixon, Richard. *1999: Victory Without War*. New York: Pocket Books, 1989.
Novak, Robert. "Worse Than Apartheid?" *Washington Post*, April 9, 2007.
Oren, Michael. *Six Days of War: June 1967 and the Making of the Modern Middle East*. New York: Medisco Press, 2003.
Peleg, Ilan. *The Legacy of George W. Bush's Foreign Policy: Moving Beyond Neoconservatism*. New York: Routledge, 2009.
Peretz, Martin and Daniel Pipes. "Bush, Clinton, & the Jews—A Debate," *Commentary*, October 1992.
Pew Poll. "How the Faithful Voted: 2012 Preliminary Analysis," November 7, 2012.
Pipes, Daniel. "Why I Just Quit the Republican Party," *Philadelphia Inquirer*, July 21, 2016.
Podhoretz, John. 3:32 P.M., March 22, 2018, Twitter.
Podhoretz, Norman. "Is the Bush Doctrine Dead?" *Commentary*, September 2006.
Podhoretz, Norman. "Pity the Palestinians? Count Me Out," in *The Wall Street Journal*, April 9, 2014.
Podhoretz, Norman. "The Neoconservative Anguish Over Reagan's Foreign Policy," *New York Times*, May 2, 1982.
Podhoretz, Norman. *Making It*. New York: Random House, 1967.
Podhoretz, Norman. *My Love Affair with America: The Cautionary Tale of a Cheerful Conservative*. New York: The Free Press, 2000.
Podhoretz, Norman. *Why Are Jews Liberal?* New York: Doubleday Books, 2009.

Podhoretz, Norman. *World War IV: The Long Struggle Against Islamo-Fascism*. New York: Doubleday, 2007.
Pollack, Noah. "Peter Beinart and the Destruction of Liberal Zionism," *Commentary*, May 1, 2010.
Pollack, Noah. "Weizmann's Answer," *Commentary*, October 8, 2007.
Prothero, Stephen. "They'll always lose the culture wars: The right loves fighting lost causes—but liberals keep winning," *Salon*, January 31, 2016.
Quealy, Kevin. "Your Rabbi? Probably a Democrat. Your Baptist Pastor? Probably a Republican. Your Priest? Who Knows," *New York Times*, June 12, 2017.
Ravid, Barak. "Netanyahu Warns Outcome of Egypt Revolution Could Be Like Iran's," *Ha'aretz*, January 31, 2011.
Ravid, Barak. "Trump: Stay Strong Israel, January 20th is Fast Approaching," *Haaretz*, December 28, 2016.
Real Clear Politics Staff. "Bill Kristol: Donald Trump Knows 'Deep in His Heart' That He Should Never Be President," *Real Clear Politics*, September 23, 2016.
Rich, Frank. "The Booing of Wolfowitz," *New York Times*, May 11, 2002.
Richman, Rick. "Netanyahu Must Give That Speech," *Commentary*, February 12, 2015.
Roberts, Paul Craig. "Massive Defeat for US Neocon Nazis and Israel's Crazed Netanyahu," *paulcraigroberts.org*, April 2, 2015.
Rosenblatt, Gary. "How the World Turned Against Israel," *Times of Israel*, May 13, 2015.
Rosner, Shmuel. "Why Israel Hates the Egyptian Uprising," *Slate*, February 3, 2011.
Rothman, Noah. "A Proper Contempt for the UN," *Commentary*, November 23, 2016.
Rubin, Jennifer. "Cut Off All Foreign Aid? That Would Be 'Dumb' and Dangerous," *Washington Post*, October 16, 2014.
Rubin, Jennifer. "Why It's Correct to Label the Obama Administration 'anti-Israel,'" *Washington Post*, January 20, 2016.
Rucker, Philip and Karen Tumulty. "Donald Trump is Holding a Government Casting Call. He's Seeking 'The Look,'" *Washington Post*, December 22, 2016.
Said, Edward. "The Myth of the 'Clash of Civilizations,'" transcript from the Media Education Foundation, 1998. https://www.mediaed.org/transcripts/Edward-Said-The-Myth-of-Clash-Civilizations-Transcript.pdf.
Salama, Vivian. "Nikki Haley Remains Boldly Off-Message at the UN," *Times of Israel*, May 1, 2017.
Schaefer, Brian. "Where Does Donald Trump Stand on Israel?" *Ha'Aretz*, November 10, 2016.
Schoenfeld, Gabriel. *The Return of Anti-Semitism*. New York: Encounter Books, 2005.
Scholem, Gershom. "Israel and the Diaspora," in *On Jews and Judaism in Crisis: Selected Essays*. New York: Paul Dry Books, 2012.
Scowcroft, Brent. "Don't Attack Iraq," *Wall Street Journal*, August 15, 2002.
Sharansky, Natan. "Antisemitism in 3-D," *Forward*, January 21, 2005.
Smith, Ben. "J Street Blames 'Neocons' . . . 'Thuggish Smear Tactics' for Conference Woes," *Politico*, October 16, 2009.
Smith, Jordan Michael. "An Unpopular Man," *The New Republic*, July 7, 2015.
Smith, Lee. "Norman Podhoretz, 89 Today, Has Made It," *Tablet*, January 16, 2019.
Smith, Stephen B. "Leo Strauss's Forgotten Letter," *Commentary*, September 13, 2016.
Sniegoski, Stephen J. *The Transparent Cabal: The Neoconservative Agenda, War in the Middle East, and the National Interest of Israel*. United States: Enigma Editions, 2008.
Sobran, Joseph. "For Fear of the Jews," Sobran.com. http://www.sobran.com/fearofjews.shtml.
Sokol, Sam. "'Institutional Anti-Semitism' Exists in the U.S., Expert Says," *Jerusalem Post*, February 19, 2015.
Stanley, Paul. "Where is Israel on Evangelical Christian Voters' List of Priorities?" *Jewish News Service* (JNS.org), August 27, 2015.
Stanley, Timothy. *The Crusader: The Life and Tumultuous Times of Pat Buchanan*. New York: Thomas Dunne Books, 2012.
Stephens, Bret. "Israel Looks Beyond America," *Wall Street Journal*, February 15, 2016.
Stephens, Bret. "The Nonsense of '50 Years of Occupation' By Israel," *Pittsburgh Post-Gazette*, June 6, 2017.

Strauss, Leo. "Why We Remain Jews," *Jewish Philosophy and the Crisis of Modernity*. New York: Study of Jewish Community Organization, 1962.

Taheri, Amir. "Is Israel the Problem?" *Commentary*, February 2007.

Tarniopolsky, Noga. "John Bolton Told Israel: Condi Rice Sold You Out; Ex-Official Says," *The Daily Beast*, March 27, 2018.

Tibon, Amir. "Trump's Secretary of State Refuses to Say Western Wall is in Israel," *Haaretz*, May 22, 2017.

Times of Israel Staff. "Northern Israeli City to Name New Park After Trump," *Times of Israel*, December 7, 2017.

Tobin, Jonathan S. "How a Court Sank Israel's Economy," *Commentary*, March 28, 2016.

Tobin, Jonathan S. "Is Nikki Haley the Alternative Secretary of State?" *National Review*, June 30, 2017.

Tobin, Jonathan S. "Hillary vs. Liberals on BDS," *Commentary*, May 10, 2016.

Tobin, Jonathan S. "Listen to the Deafening Silence," *Commentary*, October 1, 2015.

Tobin, Jonathan S. "Pinkwashing? Gay Rights Shows the Difference Between Israel and Palestinians," *Commentary*, April 20, 2012.

Tobin, Jonathan S. "Who Opposes Democracy in Israel?" *Commentary*, December 22, 2015.

Tribune News Service. "John Kerry Tears into Israel Over Settlements on His Way Out the Door," *Chicago Tribune*, December 28, 2016.

Tyrell, R. Emmett. "After Reagan Comes Trump," *The American Spectator*, September 14, 2016.

Tyrell, R. Emmett Jr. *The Conservative Crack-Up*. New York: Simon & Schuster, 1992.

UN Watch. "UN Adopts 6 Resolutions on Israel, 0 on Rest of World," November 24, 2015. http://www.unwatch.org/un-adopts-6-resolutions-on-israel-0-on-rest-of-world/.

Vidal, Gore. "The Empire Strikes Back," *The Nation*, March 22, 1986.

Waltz, Kenneth N. "Why Iran Should Get the Bomb," *Foreign Affairs*, July/August 2012.

Walzer, Michael. "Why Are Jews Liberal? (An Alternative to Norman Podhoretz)," *Dissent*, October 30, 2009.

Wanniski, Jude. "The Unanimous 9/11 Report," Lewrockwell.com, July 28, 2004.

Weiss, Philip. "The U.S. is at last facing the neocon captivity," *Mondoweiss*, May 19, 2015. http://mondoweiss.net/2015/05/facing-neocon-captivity/.

Wisse, Ruth. "Rising to the Occasion," *The Weekly Standard*, March 16, 2015.

Wisse, Ruth. "The Delegitimation of Israel," in *The Essential Neoconservative Reader*, ed. Mark Gerson. Boston, MA: Addison-Wesley Publishing Company, 1996.

Wisse, Ruth. "The Jewishness of *Commentary*," in *Commentary in American Life*, ed. Murray Friedman. Philadelphia, PA: Temple University Press, 2005.

Wisse, Ruth. *If I am Not for Myself: The Liberal Betrayal of the Jews*. New York: The Free Press, 1992.

Yassin-Kassab, Robin. "How neoconservatives led US to war in Iraq," *The National*, December 11, 2014. http://www.thenational.ae/arts-lifestyle/the-review/how-neoconservatives-led-us-to-war-in-iraq.

YouTube, Greta Van Susteran's Interview with James Traficant on Fox News, September 10, 2009. https://www.youtube.com/watch?v=0scNGzWfv8A.

Index

Abbas, Mahmoud, 43
Abrams, Elliot, 1, 25, 28, 56, 61, 72, 74, 75, 77
Abunimah, Ali, 70
Adams, Rachel, 70
Adelson, Sheldon, 62
Afghanistan, 74
Ahmad, Mohammad Indrees, 11
Alt-Right, 14
The American Conservative, 37
American Jewish Committee, 17
American Israel Public Affairs Committee, 61, 70, 73, 74, 83
Anti-Defamation League, 67
Arab Liberation Front, 27
Arab Spring, 28, 41, 42
Arafat, Suha, 69
Arafat, Yasser, 55, 69
Ashrawi, Hanan, 80
Assad, Bashar, 63, 82
The Atlantic, 28, 65, 78

Baker, James, 27, 62
Bannon, Steve, 77
Barak, Ehud, 55
Begin, Menachem, 43, 55
Berger, Peter, 5
Banfield, Edward, 5
BDS, 70
Beinart, Peter, 12, 57, 58
Ben-Ami, Jeremy, 73, 80

Bennett, William, 5, 25
Bin Laden, Osama, 57
Blumenthal, Max, 70
Blumenthal, Sidney, 70
Boehm, Omri, 14
Boehner, John, 53
Bolton, John, 24, 77, 78, 79, 80
Boot, Max, 1, 44, 63, 76, 78, 81, 82, 83
Bonjean, Ron, 62
Bradford, Mel, 37
Brandeis, Louis, 54
Breitbart, Andrew, 10
Breitbart, 10
Brooks, David, 1
Buchanan, Pat, 7, 8, 9, 11, 24, 25, 30, 37, 38, 39, 41, 44, 45, 46
Buckley, William F, 8, 9
Burnham, James, 9
Bush, George H. W., 9, 27, 80
Bush, George W, 6, 7, 25, 27, 31, 33, 37, 41, 42, 64, 72, 77, 83
Bush, Jeb, 62

Carter, Jimmy, 18, 55, 56, 66, 83
Chambers, Whittaker, 9
Cheney, Dick, 24
China, 30, 55, 74, 82
Chronicles, 9, 37
Chomsky, Noam, 12, 83
Churchill, Winston, 25
City College of New York, 8

Clean Break Paper, 24, 25
Clinton, Bill, 25, 33
Clinton, Hillary, vii, 61, 63, 64, 65, 66, 69, 70, 71, 72, 83
CNN, 10
Cohen, Elliot, 17, 19, 49
Commentary, 1, 5, 9, 17, 18, 19, 27, 31, 32, 33, 49, 52, 53, 55, 70, 77, 79, 81
Congressional Black Caucus, 18
Coulter, Ann, 40
Cuba, 30, 74

de Borchgrave, Arnaud, 25
Declaration of the Establishment of the State of Israel, 84
Decter, Midge, 1, 8, 15, 18, 30, 42, 66, 84
Demjanjuk, John, 38
Dershowitz, Alan, 38
Dissent, 6
Dreyfus Affair, 15
Drury, Shadia, 6

East Jerusalem, 58
Egypt, 28, 31, 41, 42, 71, 75, 76, 79, 84
Eichmann, Adolph, 18
Emanuel, Rahm, 38
Emergency Committee for Israel, 74
Erdogan, Recep Tayyip, 82
Eshkol, Levi, 31

Face the Nation, 18
Family Research Council, 67
Farrakhan, Louis, 18
Feith, Douglas, 1, 24
Findlay, Paul, 5
Finklestein, Norman, 12, 41, 83
First Things, 9
Fleischer, Ari, 65
Flynn, Michael, 77
Foreign Affairs, 74
The Forward, 23
Foxman, Abraham, 38, 67
FOX News, 11, 77
Francis, Samuel, 37
French, David, 81
Friedman, David, 72, 75
Frum, David, 1, 8, 77, 78
Fukuyama, Francis, 5

Gallagher, Mike, 81
Gaza, 41, 55, 57, 58, 68, 80
Gershman, Carl, 18, 19
Gillerman, Dan, 78
Glasner, Moshe Shmuel, 16
Glazer, Nathan, 11, 18, 23
Glick, Caroline, 76
Goldberg, Jeffrey, 28
Goldberg, Jonah, 81
Goldberg, Michelle, 10
Gordon, Evelyn, 52
Gorka, Sebastian, 77
Gottfried, Paul, viii, 37, 38, 39, 40, 41, 43, 44, 46, 49, 52, 75
Greenblatt, Jason, 72
Greenbaum, Daniela, 81
Gulf War, 8, 9

Ha'aretz, 43
Haley, Nikki, 80, 81, 82, 83
Halkin, Hillel, 1
Hamas, 41, 43, 55, 70, 72
Harries, Owen, 29
Harpers, 84
Helms, Jesse, 77
Heritage Foundation, 8, 30, 42
Herman, Arthur, 52
Herzl, Theodor, 14, 15
Herzog, Isaac, 61
Hess, Moses, 14, 15
Hezbollah, 41, 55
Himmelfarb, Gertrude, 66
Horowitz, David, 1, 10
Huntington, Samuel, 68
Hussein, Saddam, 27, 63

India, 71
Institute for the Study of Global Anti-Semitism, 14
Iraq, 25, 26, 27, 31, 64, 74, 83
Iraq War, 26, 64, 83
Iran, 25, 26, 32, 33, 41, 53, 66, 68, 71, 79, 83, 84
ISIS, 30

Jabotinsky, Vladimir, 14, 15
Jackson, Henry, 1, 72
Jackson, Jesse, 11
January 25 Revolution, 28

Index

Jerusalem Post, 40, 76
Jewish Home Party, 76
Jewish National Fund, 65
Jinping, Xi, 82
Johnson, Lyndon, 31
Joint Comprehensive Plan of Action on Iran, 71, 79, 83
Jordan, 75, 84
J Street, 70, 73, 80

Kadima, 45
Kagan, Donald, 1
Kagan, Robert, 1, 25, 31, 33, 63, 64, 83
Kalischer, Zvi Hersch, 16
Kaplan, Fred, 25
Kesler, Charles, 29
Kerry, John, 46, 57, 58
King Salman of Saudia Arabia, 25
Kirk, Russell, 8, 37
Kirkpatrick, Jeanne, 5, 31
Kissinger, Henry, 8, 29, 30, 31, 33
Klein, Joe, 75
Klein, Naomi, 12
Kook, Abraham Isaac, 16
Kozodoy, Neal, 17, 19
Kramer, Martin, 10, 74
Krauthammer, Charles, 1, 8, 16, 27, 58
Kristol, Irving, 1, 8, 18, 29, 30, 39, 45, 46, 49, 66
Kristol, William, 1, 10, 25, 33, 53, 62, 63, 75, 77, 78, 81
Kudlow, Larry, 77
Kurds, 55
Kushner, Jared, 72

Labor Party, 41
Lebanon, 41, 43, 78
Lerner, Michael, 70
Lewis, Anthony, 54
Lewis, Bernard, 68
Lieberman, Joseph, 1
Likud, 1, 24, 25, 28, 39, 41, 45, 50
Lindbergh, Charles, 8

Marx, Karl, 15
McConnell, Scott, 7
McGovern, George, 72
The McLaughlin Group, 8
McMaster, H. R., 77

McMullin, Evan, 63
Mearsheimer, John, 5, 10, 26, 41
Meir, Golda, 29, 31, 55
Mercer, Ilana, 39
Merkel, Angela, 28
Morgenthau, Hans, 29
Moynihan, Daniel Patrick, 5
MSNBC, 63
Mubarek, Hosni, 28
Muravchik, Joshua, viii, 1, 18, 30, 37, 38, 43, 54, 55, 56, 63, 70, 83
Muslim Brotherhood, 28

Nasser, Abdul, 31
The National Interest, 29
National Review, 7, 9, 39, 81
Netanyahu, Benjamin, 18, 24, 27, 28, 32, 41, 53, 61, 62, 65, 70, 71, 75, 79, 80
Neuhaus, Richard John, 9
New York Times, 14, 66, 70, 75
Nixon, Richard, 7, 29, 30, 31
Novak, Robert, 7, 37
The Nation, 23
Nuterei Karta, 12, 13

Obama, Barack, 11, 25, 32, 53, 57, 63, 65, 67, 74, 75, 76, 79
Old New Land, 15
Olmert, Ehud, 41, 42, 43, 55, 78
Operation Defensive Shield, 31
Oren, Michael, 65
Osirak Reactor, 26, 31
O'Sullivan, John, 9

Palestinian Authority, 71, 72
Palestinian Liberation Organization, 18, 27, 55, 80
Paul, Rand, 74
Peleg, Ilan, 45, 46
Peretz, Martin, 27
Perle, Richard, 1, 8, 24, 25
Pergola, Sergio Della, 58
Perkins, Tony, 67
Pipes, Daniel, 10, 27, 63, 71
Pinsker, Leo, 15
Podhoretz, John, 1, 19, 27, 63, 77, 78
Podhoretz, Norman, viii, 1, 6, 7, 9, 17, 18, 19, 29, 31, 38, 39, 41, 42, 50, 53, 61, 66, 67, 69

Politico, 73
Pollard, Jonathan, 27
Pompeo, Mike, 80
Powell, Colin, 26
Priebus, Reince, 72
Putin, Vladimir, 44, 71, 82

Reagan, Ronald, 6, 8, 9, 31, 66, 72
Republican Jewish Coalition, 65
Resolution 1701, 78
Rice, Condoleezza, 43, 78
Richman, Rich, 33
Roberts, Paul Craig, 7
Rockwell, Lew, 37
Rome and Jerusalem, 15
Romney, Mitt, 67
Rosner, Shmuel, 28
Rostow, Eugene, 56
Rothman, Noah, 81
Rubin, Jennifer, 67
Rumsfeld, Donald, 5, 25
Ryn, Claes, 37, 75

Said, Edward, 68, 69, 83
Sanders, Bernie, 67
Sasse, Ben, 81
Saudi Arabia, 25, 30, 71, 72
Schoenfeld, Gabriel, 38
Scholem, Gershom, 12
Schultz, George, 33
Schumer, Chuck, 83
Scowcroft, Brent, 27
Shah of Iran, 41
Shaked, Ayelet, 76
Shamir, Yitzhak, 27, 55
Sharansky, Natan, 23, 24
Sharon, Ariel, 25, 26, 31, 41, 55
Shults, Tammie Jo, 81
Sinai Peninsula, 31
Six Day War, 18, 43
Slate, 10, 25
Sniegoski, Stephen J, 5, 24, 41
Sobran, Joseph, 7, 9, 37
Soros, George, 73
The Spokesman Review, 54
Steinfels, Peter, 6
Stephens Bret, 1, 41, 43, 63, 71, 72, 76, 77
Straits of Tiran, 31
Strauss, Leo, 6, 9, 13, 38

Suez Canal, 31
Susteren, Greta Van, 11
Syria, 30, 31, 78, 83, 84

Taheri, Amir, 32
Theodoracopulos, Taki, 37
Tikkun, 70
Tillerson, Rex, 72, 76, 80, 82
Times of Israel, 43
Tobin, Jonathan, 1, 32, 51, 52, 62
Tonsor, Stephen, 37
Toynbee, Arnold, 14
Traficant, James, 11, 38
Trump, Donald, vii, 10, 14, 61, 63, 64, 65, 66, 69, 71, 72, 75, 76, 77, 78, 80, 81, 83
Turkey, 71, 82
Two State Solution, 58, 79
Tyler Force Act, 71
Tyrell, R. Emmett, 5, 66

Uganda Plan, 15

Vidal, Gore, 23

Washington Post, 7, 24, 56, 64, 67, 74, 78
Washington Times, 25, 44
The Weekly Standard, 1, 16, 53, 55, 72, 77, 78, 81
Wall Street Journal, 57
Walt, Stephen, 5, 10, 26, 41
Waltz, Kenneth, 32
Walzer, Michael, 6
Wanniski, Jude, 57
West Bank, 58, 75
Wisse, Ruth, 19, 32, 54, 56, 57
Weiss, Philip, 5, 43
Weizmann, Chaim, 15
Wilkerson, Lawrence, 26
Wolfowitz, Paul, 1, 25, 42
Women of the Wall, 52
Wurmster, David, 24

Yassin-Kassab, Robin, 11
Yom Kippur War, 29, 31
Young, Andrew, 18, 19

Zionist Union, 61

About the Author

Adam L. Fuller, PhD, is associate professor of politics and international relations at Youngstown State University. He is the author of *Taking the Fight to the Enemy: Neoconservatism and the Age of Ideology* (2012).

www.ingramcontent.com/pod-product-compliance
Lightning Source LLC
Chambersburg PA
CBHW020130010526
44115CB00008B/1050